An Owner's Guide To the Human Body.

An Easy to Understand Overview Of the Body and How to Best Use It.

By Dr. Jim Walkenbach, D.C.

D
JW Publishing, Inc.
Bow, WA

Dedication

This book is dedicated to the memory of my late son, Brian, a kind, gentle spirit who helped me more than he could ever know. His entire family and all his friends miss him tremendously. Brian will always be in our hearts, minds, and souls. We love you, Brian!

An Owner's Guide

Table of Contents

An Owner's Guide

Introduction

There is a saying in architecture that states, "Form follows function." That saying applies to all designs, including the body and its systems. It is easy for me to look at the body in terms of form following function with my engineering degree and my chiropractic training. The combination has held me in good stead for many years. In this book, I intend to present a guide to the body's systems and how we can best support them.

Each time I have spoken before groups numerous questions have arisen regarding health in general, and nutrition in particular. My explanations of how the body was designed have intrigued most audiences and I have been asked repeatedly if I had a book on all the information I have about health. My answer was always "No," everything was in my head.

A dear friend has told me several times of a saying her aunt used: "If three people tell you you're drunk, you'd better lie down." Well, many, many people have told me I ought to write a book about my knowledge of the human body and how it maintains itself.

This is the book. I thank everyone who has ever heard me and asked me to write a book. You may ask yourself, "How does this book apply to me?" My response is it applies to anyone who wants general information on how the body was designed to work, and how to best help himself or herself.

You will read several statements about how chiropractic can help someone with a given problem. I grew up in a chiropractic family and became a chiro-practor because of what I saw and experienced per-sonally. Every reference where I mention the possi-bility of chiropractic helping a person with a specific condition, brings with it at least one personal expe-rience with a patient in my practice. To do anything else would be a loss of integrity for me, knowing what I know. This is not to say that chiropractic can cure anything. No healthcare practitioner cures any-thing. The body heals itself with the help of the healthcare practitioner.

I have taken numerous seminars on nutrition and health over the years since I graduated from Logan Chiropractic College. The two most influential peo-ple in my education of nutrition are Dr. M. Ted Morter, Jr., D.C., and Dr. Bert Hanicke, D.C. I will refer the reader to three books written by Dr. Morter for further investigation and understanding of the biochemistry of the body. They are: "Correlative Urinalysis: The Body Knows Best," "Chiropractic Physiology," and "pH, Your Potential for Health."

Life is about Choices

One of the most important things I can tell anyone about life is that everything about life is a choice. You have choices about what you eat, drink, smoke, breathe, and how you exercise, if at all. The thing about choices is that with each choice come associ-ated lessons. Some of the lessons are enjoyable and some are painful. It is up to each of us to learn the lessons and then either make new choices, or stick with the choices that worked for us.

The body makes choices based on sensory input. It has ten times more sensory nerves coming from the periphery and going to the brain, than it does motor nerves coming from the brain and going to the muscles and organs. This seems to indicate the body is demanding a lot of information from the peripheral senses, which is true. The brain is a good computer that wants as much information as possible before making choices.

Something "New"

We normally assume the five senses are the only means available to the body to get input. There is another sensing "organ" the body has that medical textbooks do not talk about. It is the body's electromagnetic field, sometimes called the "aura."

With that enticing concept and so many others to be covered, it is difficult to decide where to begin. Why not begin with a brief description of the systems of the body and then move on to how the embryo develops some of those systems?

An Owner's Guide

Chapter 1
Body Systems

Respiratory System

This system is used to bring oxygen into the body and eliminate carbon dioxide. Sensors, which measure the level of oxygen and carbon dioxide in the blood stream, trigger the respiratory centers in the nervous system causing an increased rate of breathing when the oxygen level is too low, and/or the carbon dioxide level is too high. Oxygen is one of the important elements used by the body for energy production. Without it, we perish.

Problems with breathing primarily come from allergies, neurological miscommunication (asthma), smoking, inhaling fumes from toxic substances, and traumatic wounds. Lack of oxygen can play a role in one's ability to maintain consciousness or even think clearly. It can contribute to increased blood pressure as the body tries to bring more oxygen to the brain, which can be a factor in headaches.

The more oxygen we can bring to the cells on a regular basis aids the body in maintaining homeostasis (in essence the status quo of the body.) Most people do not breathe deeply enough and the result is lethargy or a sense of not being able to think clearly. This is why most people will feel more energetic after a "workout."

1

The Skin

Another organ of respiration is the skin. If all the pores of the body were somehow sealed shut, the person would be heavily taxed to breathe in enough oxygen. This is one of the reasons to get outside and exercise.

The skin is also the largest organ of elimination. Toxins are released through the skin, especially when the intestinal system and kidneys are not functioning properly. Most people consider acne to be a "bacterial" problem, which is partially true. Bacteria are opportunistic organisms. Everyone has bacteria on their skin at all times. When the pores of the skin are being used to eliminate toxins, a beneficial environment exists for the breeding of bacteria. The bacteria do their thing and are blamed for the problem.

Actually, if one suffers from severe acne, it would be beneficial to improve the elimination of the intestinal system and the kidneys. The largest contributing factor to poor elimination is poor digestion of foods, and excessive fat/protein intake. Another factor can be the hormonal changes teenagers go through. This has an effect on eating habits and digestive capability.

When the body cannot digest foods properly, carbohydrates ferment, fats become rancid, and proteins putrefy. The end products are toxins that need to be eliminated. If the system that is designed to handle the problem is overwhelmed, the skin is the "fallback" or emergency relief position for elimination. As these toxins are pushed through the pores, it is easy for pores to become blocked and create the acidic environment which bacteria love.

I suggest adding digestive enzymes to the diet to assist in breaking down fats and proteins. Essential fatty acids can also be beneficial, for the body needs fatty acids in order to make proper hormones, and the "good" cholesterol. The good cholesterol aids in digesting other fats and eliminating them in the normal waste removal systems. Consequently, I recommend a high quality flax seed oil to support this process. Supplementation with vitamin "A" is also beneficial, with a minimum of 10,000 IU's per day. Vitamin "A" supports the liver in the process of detoxification and also aids directly with the skin and the capillaries in the skin.

Body odor is another example of eliminating toxins. Odors are most usually found in a part of the fats called (not so surprisingly) aromatic rings. The aroma of garlic comes from the fats of the garlic. When someone consumes large quantities of garlic they often smell like garlic. Primarily, cooked, or roasted garlic gives off this offensive odor. Raw garlic has less potential for odors because raw garlic is more digestible than cooked garlic. Garlic supplements often have the fats removed, leading to the term "odorless" garlic.

The odors coming from proteins usually come from poor digestion of amino acids containing sulfur. The sulfur is converted to hydrogen sulfide, or the familiar term and smell of "rotten eggs."

The skin plays yet another role in the human body. It is a pathway of absorption for nutrients and toxins both.   One of the toxins that many people in our society readily apply to their skin is anti-perspirant deodorant. You may be shocked to learn the reason that anti-perspirants work is that aluminum in anti-perspirants actually poisons the nerve endings that go to the sweat glands. While poisoned, the nerves do not signal the glands to release perspiration. Aluminum has an affinity to nervous tissue including the brain and is associated with Alzheimer's and Parkinson's diseases.   Some alternative healthcare providers believe the increasing numbers of Alzheimer's patients is a result of aluminum cook-ware used in the 50's -60's, and the ever-increasing use of anti-perspirants.

(It might be interesting to look at the statistics of Alzheimer's, Parkinson's and breast cancer in soci-eties that use anti-perspirants, and compare those numbers with numbers from societies that use less of the product.   The use of aluminum cookware would have to be factored in there as well.)

There are reasons for using gloves when dealing with solvents and other toxic chemicals.   Solvents are readily absorbed through the skin and can affect the nervous system.   For example, PCP began as an industrial solvent and eventually was added to the list of chemicals drug addicts used for increased drug effects. Marijuana laced with PCP became popular in the 60's and 70's and continues on and off today. PCP can cause severe reactions in the body and the user may become extremely violent.

I heard of a case where a police unit raided a drug lab and a person making PCP threw a beaker of the substance in a policeman's face.   It was absorbed immediately through the skin. The policeman had to be restrained by several of his fellow officers and taken to a hospital. The residue of PCP is difficult to metabolize and is eventually stored in the body's fat cells. Any strong physical or emotional activity can cause residues to be re-released into the blood stream resulting in hallucinations and aberrant, violent behavior. (This is what "flashbacks" are all about with marijuana, PCP, and LSD.) Because of the exposure, the officer had to be medically retired from the force.

On a positive note, application of nutrients to the skin can be an effective means of absorption. Some in the health field believe vitamin "E" can be absorbed more efficiently through the skin than through taking a capsule orally. Vitamin "E" applied to scars can thin or possibly eliminate scar tissue. Any of the vitamins that are in oil form may be applied in this manner.

We see commercials for nicotine patches to help smokers wean themselves from smoking. There are estrogen patches for hormone replacement and potentially hormonal patches for birth control. It is certain more skin absorption procedures will be used in the future.

The absorption of one mineral can be used as an indicator as to potential deficiency of that mineral. You apply a one-inch square of tincture of iodine to the fold of the elbow and then observe how long it takes for the iodine to disappear. If the iodine is absorbed in less than 24 hours, the person might be low in iodine. If the iodine disappears in less than 12 hours, it is suggested the person is quite deficient in iodine. Iodine is used along with thyroid hormones and is essential for proper metabolic activity. The normal blood tests for thyroid function rarely find deficiency of iodine, yet the World Health Organization has stated that as many as 70% to 80% of the world population is deficient in iodine. If one uses this test and there is indication of iodine deficiency, supplementation of kelp can bring the iodine levels of the body up. Later tests will then show the iodine stain remaining for 24 hours or more.

Nervous Systems

Note that there are more than one nervous system. The main classifications are the **sensory** system comprising the "data" input to the brain and its centers, the **central** system consisting of the brain and spinal cord, and **motor** system, which carries the command information from the brain to the muscles and organs. There is also the autonomic nervous system which controls the visceral (gut, organ, and glandular) functions of the body and is divided into sympathetic and parasympathetic systems.

Everything in the body is controlled either directly or indirectly by the nervous systems of the body. Even hormonal control is responsive to nervous system input.

There are too many conditions associated with the nervous system to mention in a book like this. Realize that because the body is controlled by the nervous system, it is imperative the system function without interference. This is the primary reason for chiropractic care. Dr. Su, at the University of

Colorado's biophysics department, has shown that as little as 4mm. of mercury pressure on a nerve will cause it to malfunction. You can apply that much pressure with a feather!

The sympathetic and parasympathetic nerves have both stimulatory and inhibitory effects depending on the gland. If these nerves malfunction by pressure causing an over stimulation of nerve signals, spasms and cramping in muscles, and excessive secretions from glands can occur; or the exact opposite if pressure causes inhibition of nerve signals, inability to use muscles effectively, and reduced secretions from glands can occur.

Musculo-Skeletal System

Our muscles and bones allow us to move. Some bones like the skull and spine also encase important tissues, i.e., the brain and spinal cord. The Design Engineer of the body did a fantastic job allowing us to evolve into an upright creature.

We can assume from our structure that the brain and the spinal cord are the most critical of the body's systems because they are encased in bone. The next most critical would be the body's organs, protected by the rig cage.

The spine has three normal curves to it if you look at it from the side. There is the "cervical" (neck) forward curve, the "thoracic" (mid-back) posterior curve, and the "lumbar" (low-back) forward curve. Some consider the "sacrum" to be a fourth curve that is posterior in orientation. The establishment of these curves allows the structure of the body to

7

carry sixteen times more weight than it could if the spine were a straight column from front to back.

If the spine is in a balanced state and remains flexible, there is minimal interference with the nerves that exit the spine. This is the goal of chiropractic care. Damage can occur very early in life with symptoms not becoming evident until middle age.

A study of young football players was done in Nebraska, in the 1970's. The group was followed for 5 years from the ages of 7 to 12. X-rays were taken at the beginning of the study and at the end. At the end, 50% of the children showed permanent cervical spinal damage that was evident on x-ray.

Life is about choices and football and other sports are part of the selection of choices. The body was not designed to take the punishment football can inflict on it. I was not allowed to play football in high school because my father, a chiropractor, said men my size, 6'7" and 230 lbs. are too susceptible to knee injuries. So, I proved him right by having three knee operations at West Point, one from playing football, one from basketball, and one from baseball. When I graduated from West Point in 1969, and had my Army induction physical, the orthopedic surgeons told me I had 80-year-old knees!

The skeletal system is the framework to which the muscles attach. Virtually all muscles cross over joints and this is what allows us to be able to move.

Problems arise from trauma, toxicity, and disease. Misalignments of the spine affect the body's nervous system and therefore all the muscles and organs

8

controlled by those affected nerves. If fractures are not healed in proper alignment, limited range of motion can result. Both toxicity and trauma can damage the bones causing arthritis. Some autoimmune diseases like rheumatoid arthritis or lupus damage bones and joints causing decreased mobility.

Due to the ingenuity of the being, people have developed the modern prosthetic devices that can allow some people who would otherwise be wheelchair bound, to actually run in competition. Others have developed arm and hand prostheses for upper extremity amputees. Hip and knee replacements have become commonplace now and allow the formerly incapacitated person to regain his/her mobility. (I am thinking about mine now.)

The muscles are considered "soft" tissue. Without the use of muscles we would not be able to move, as some diseases point out so painfully. Muscles, like bones, are susceptible to problems from trauma, toxicity, and disease. Proper nutrition and exercise are important to maintain good muscle function. The Standard American Diet (better known as SAD) does not provide a balanced nutritional intake to maintain any of the body's systems properly. This deficiency is most often seen in the musculo-skeletal system of overweight children and adults. Osteoporosis is one of the nutritional concerns becoming epidemic in our society because of SAD.

Some diseases like MS and MD may have a neurological and/or autoimmune component. There are some nutritional products that may assist with many of these debilitating diseases to slow the progress and minimize the symptoms. Fibromyalgia is considered by some to be epidemic. I mention some possible products that may assist these sufferers later in the book.

Circulatory System

The heart, arteries, arterioles, capillaries, veins, and venules comprise the circulatory system. The arterial side of the system carries oxygenated blood from the heart to the periphery (the body). The venus system carries the blood from the periphery back to the heart. The heart is actually two pumps. One side (right) pumps the returning blood into the lungs, and the other side (left) pumps the oxygenated blood from the lungs to the body.

The liver, kidneys, and spleen act as blood cleaners, with the liver and kidneys being the primary agents. The liver has the responsibility of removing most of the toxins from the blood stream. This includes drug residues, inhaled or absorbed toxins, byproducts of poor digestion, and poisoning by alcohol. As one desires to improve his/her health, the first stage of improvement has to be detoxifying and supporting the liver in this process.

The kidneys are responsible for filtering the blood, removing anything non-beneficial that is water soluble, and recycling anything beneficial. The "bicarbonate ion" is the most important beneficial entity recycled.

This bicarbonate ion is part of the body's defense against acids. It is reformed with sodium to make sodium bicarbonate. The sodium does not come from table salt (ionic bonding, very strong, physiologically useless), but from fruits and vegetables (covalent bonding, easily broken, physiologically useful). Without sufficient sodium, the body has a difficult time handling all the acids produced by muscle activity, ingested and inhaled toxins, and drug residues. When there is insufficient sodium available, the body has to improvise. The body takes the largest available alkaline mineral, calcium, from bones and muscle tissue and combines it with the bicarbonate ion. If this sounds like "osteoporosis," it is. Calcium bicarbonate is not as efficient as sodium bicarbonate and more of it is needed when the sodium level is insufficient to meet the need.

The spleen eliminates weak red blood cells and recycles hemoglobin from damaged cells. The spleen also plays a role in eliminating parasites, viruses, and bacteria. The loss of the spleen from traumatic injuries places added pressure on the liver and immune system.

Digestive System and Alimentary Tract

The digestive system and alimentary tract begin in the mouth where some digestive enzymes are released, especially for carbohydrates. The alimentary tract is similar to the "hole" in a doughnut. The alimentary tract is actually a passageway through the physical dimensions of the body without becoming a part of the internal cellular structure of the body. Anything that is in this tube, which is created from the mouth to the anus, is technically "outside" the body, like a doughnut hole.

The mouth also has sensors which signal when proteins are being consumed. These signals are sent to the parietal cells of the stomach to secrete hydrochloric acid, which is needed in the pre-digestion of those proteins.

Most people think the stomach is a rather passive entity. In fact, it is quite a mixer and masher. The stomach performs early stages of digestion and passes the chyme (that's what physiologists and biochemists call the "stuff" coming out of the stomach) into the duodenum.

Depending on the pH of the chyme and other factors, bile from the liver and gall bladder are released to assist in fat digestion. Other digestive enzymes are released from the pancreas and other areas of the small intestine.

Nutrients are absorbed through the gut wall and sent around to the body. The portal vein takes the absorbed materials to the liver to remove toxins as best it can immediately. These toxins are in the form of preservatives in the foods we eat, fats that are not easily digested, long chain amino acids, (Which are considered "foreign proteins," or poison, by the body.) yeasts, "critters" such as parasites, and whatever else we ingest, including prescription and/or recreational drugs.

Having gone through the small intestine, the chyme now passes through the "ileocecal valve." This one-way valve can be stuck open or closed, causing tendencies for diarrhea or constipation. If it is stuck closed, then distention of the small intestine and absorption of toxic materials occurs from the decaying of chyme caused by fermentation of carbohy-drates, rancidity of fats, and putrefaction of pro-teins.

This "sticking" of the ileocecal valve can be a result of toxic "shock" to the nerves controlling the valve, or mechanical disturbance to the nerves by misalign-ments of the spine and pelvis.

Water is progressively removed along the large intestine and waste matter becomes firmer, finally exiting the body through the anus. If the body sens-es something severely toxic, like salmonella, or other poisons, the water extraction is reversed and the large intestine is flooded to dilute the toxins and cause rapid expulsion, i.e., diarrhea.

Diarrhea can be a "good" thing. It is a reflex sur-vival mechanism to eliminate toxins. When it occurs, one might consider determining "why" diar-rhea is occurring, rather than just taking something to "stop" it. If the body chooses to eliminate some-thing in this manner, chances are, it needs to be eliminated.

Excessive diarrhea can be a medical emergency. Diarrhea is a "symptom" of something else going on. To stop the diarrhea before the body has finished removing the toxins, just keeps the toxins in the body.

In general, diarrhea for more than one or two days needs medical attention. If it is severe and uncon-trollable, i.e., one cannot even get to the bathroom without eliminating, then medical assistance should be sought immediately.

Diarrhea can be the result of mechanical irritation of the nerves controlling the activities of the intestinal system. This is something a chiropractor may be able to help alleviate.

Hormonal System

Hormones are chemicals released from one cell that have an effect on other cells in the body. Most people think of the sex hormones when the term "hormone" is used. In actuality, the sexual hormones are just some of the numerous hormones produced by several glands in the body.
Hormones are produced in the pituitary gland, thyroid and parathyroid glands, adrenal glands, pancreas, and the testes and ovaries.

Hormones are designed to control numerous functions in the body including growth rates, cell maturation, metabolic rate (how fast you burn calories), blood sugar concentrations, reproduction, and many, many more.

Tumors in the various glands can produce excessive secretions of certain hormones, as well as cessation of production. To a much lesser extent, mechanical disturbance of the nerves going to the glands can affect the glands function. This is how chiropractic can help alleviate hormonal problems.

Immune System

The immune system is called the "reticuloendothelial" system in physiology. That is why we call it the immune system. There are two primary ways the body defends itself from bacteria, viruses, and foreign proteins. The first method is "phagocytosis." This occurs in the bone marrow, spleen, liver, and lymph nodes. Endothelial cells are relatively "primitive" cells from an embryological standpoint and have the capability to differentiate (change) into many other types of cells. These cells directly attack bacteria, viruses, and foreign proteins.

The second method of protection from foreign invaders is the process of developing "immunity" to the invading toxin. This is done by lymphocytes. The invader is usually a protein, polysaccharide, or mucopolysaccharide. Specific cells sense the invader, and in essence make a "template" of the invader, or part of it. This template is carried to another type of cell that then manufactures thousands of molecules, which can adhere to the invader and eliminate it. This takes time.

If the body is unable to make a successful molecule or cell to defeat the invader, the body may develop an "allergy" to the toxin. Subsequent exposures to the toxic invader can result in serious reactions within the body, which progress in severity even to include death.

Most of us have known someone who has a severe allergy to bee stings. The venom (foreign protein) of the sting triggers reactions within the body, which can produce enough fluids in the lungs and airways to prevent breathing. This is what occurs during "anaphylactic shock." Another example would be if someone is allergic to penicillin or other drugs and those drugs are mistakenly administered to the person.

The immune system is supported by vitamins and minerals which are used as reserves (or specialized weapons) while fighting the battle with the toxins. Virtually all toxins are acidic. In order to help neutralize the toxins, the body needs molecules that can counterbalance the acidity. Antioxidants are those molecules. We know many of them like vitamins "A," "C," "E," and minerals like selenium, and other molecules like bioflavinoids, or pycnogenol.

The body's primary antioxidant is glutathione, produced inside the cells themselves. Glutathione is composed of three essential amino acids. If one takes glutathione as a supplement, the three essential amino acids are metabolized into other amino acids the body needs to repair itself, or otherwise function normally. I address the importance of glutathione much more, later in the book. Suffice it to say glutathione makes the other antioxidants more effective, protects cell walls from attack by viruses and free radicals, and allows the liver to convert fat-soluble toxins into water-soluble toxins for elimination by the kidneys.

The immune system needs the support of antioxidants in order to perform its job of protecting the body. Antibiotics are overused in our society today, making many bacteria drug-resistant. The best way anyone can avoid the need for antibiotics is to strengthen and improve his/her own immune system with proper eating and supplementation with vitamins and other antioxidants.

Chapter 2
The Cellular Beginning

We talked about the body's systems, but how were the systems developed? Embryology is the study of the embryo (beginning group of cells) and gives us information about how the body performs its tasks of growth, repair, and survival, and how it builds its systems to perform those functions.

Nervous System First

The first system the embryo develops is the nervous system. It has to start somewhere, but is there a reason why the nervous system would be first? The concept of ten times the number of sensory nerves coming from the peripheral senses seems like a good reason, and is not the only reason.

How Tissue Chooses to be Kidney

One researcher, Prof. Irwin Korr, who has primarily done his work in the osteopathic field, has shown that nerves tell the tissues of the body what type of tissue to become. His work showed nerves that go to the tongue or kidney for instance, actually tell the cells of the tongue and kidney how they are to differentiate (choose) to become tongue and kidney tissue. This "instructing" of the cells is accomplished by sending proteins, which move slowly (days) down the axon (cable) of the nerves to the synapses (connections of nerves to tissue cells). Prof. Korr gained this information by severing the nervous attachment to the organs while the tissues were still forming and finding that the cellular differentiation (choosing)

17

stopped. When reattached, the differentiation would once again progress. He also showed that if nerves that were designed to go to the kidney were attached to other tissue, then the cells of that tissue would begin to become kidney tissue cells.

For me, Prof. Korr's work is fascinating and enlightening. It tells us how manipulation of the spine, and subsequent relieving of pressure on the nerves, can affect other areas of the body. This is so, because the nerves of the body can be affected most easily as they exit their bony covering, the spinal column. A nerve, which has as little as 4 mm of mercury pressure on it, can be affected. When a nerve is affected, it can only do one of two things; over react, or under react. It cannot react normally. Consequently, pressure on the nerves that go to the parietal cells of the stomach can cause the cells to secrete too much, or not enough hydrochloric acid for digestion.

Adrenal Glands

The adrenal glands of the fetus begin to develop in the last trimester of the pregnancy. This may seem relatively innocuous, but it tells a tale as well. There are some mothers who state they feel better during the last trimester of their pregnancy. Granted, it is not a large number, but it is still significant. Most mothers are feeling worn out and tired and wanting the pregnancy to be over as soon as possible.

Why would some mothers feel better during such a period? The answer lies in the fact that some mothers are actually drawing some of the infant's adrenal secretions from the infant to themselves. In

18

essence, the infant is supplying the mother with energy she might otherwise not have.

The result of this situation is the mother may want more children, and the distinct possibility exists that the child may be born with adrenal exhaustion. The child with adrenal exhaustion may not develop rapidly and may be otherwise prone to upset or irritation.

Adrenal Exhaustion Test

There is a relatively simple test that will give one an indication as to whether or not his/her adrenal glands have been worn out, abused, over stimulated, or whatever word or phrase you would like to use. The test is done by looking in the mirror at the iris of one eye and shining a penlight into that eye. The iris of the eye will close down because of the light. Continue shining the light in the eye and see if the iris starts to "flutter" or begin to open and then close and open and close. If the iris "flutters," the adrenal glands are in need of help.

What needs to be done to assist the adrenal glands is to provide a nutritional supplementation of a high quality "Stress 'B' complex." "B" vitamins must be taken in a balanced complex for the best benefit to the body because they work synergistically (in action with each other). Raw adrenal gland supplementation may also be beneficial.

In addition, any stimulation of the adrenal glands by caffeine or nicotine should be considered for elimination. Without reduction in outside influences like caffeine, or nicotine, a person is fighting an uphill battle. Realize, addictions to these drugs of choice are not easy to eliminate. Adrenal exhaustion is a good reason to at least attempt to stop them.

Chapter 3
Energy from our Food

Digestion

Almost everyone knows of the term "digestion," but what is it? Digestion is the process of breaking down various types of foods into building blocks, to be used as fuel for our cells to run on, or to utilize for growth and/or repair.

The three food types are, of course, carbohydrates, fats, and proteins. (Do not confuse these with the four food groups in a bachelor's refrigerator I once heard a comedian describe: fast, frozen, spoiled and rotten.) The body is an engine that runs on primary and alternative fuels. It is designed to run on carbohydrates as its primary fuel, but can run on fats and proteins as the alternative fuel.

Carbohydrates

What is a carbohydrate? Basically, a carbohydrate is a molecule containing one or more sugar molecules. There are two basic forms of carbohydrates: "complex" and "refined." Quite simply, "complex" carbohydrates are those in a more natural state, coming from their source of fruits, vegetables, and whole grains. They contain important factors which assist in metabolism. "Refined" carbohydrates are those that have been processed prior to consumption and lose some of the beneficial factors; the biggest offender being refined sugar, which is pure "sucrose". Sucrose is a final stage sugar in the body's metabolism of carbohydrates. Refined carbo-

21

hydrates enter the body in a form the body would not normally be exposed to until later in the digestive process, had they been eaten raw.

Refined carbohydrates are far less preferable to the body because they are missing important metabolism co-factors. These co-factors make digestion of carbohydrates easier, and therefore healthier. Some refined carbohydrates are actually chemically treated; for example, white bread contains bleached flour. Few people ever really think about that, because all they see is the end product, which seems to have a soft texture and pleasant white color. What they do not realize is the flour is actually treated with bleach! Now how many people would apply bleach to food they were going to eat?

Refined carbohydrates, especially sucrose, are "pure" fuel. They are analogous to throwing high-octane gasoline on a fire. They want to be burned immediately. The deleterious affect they have on the body occurs only when the body cannot burn the fuels immediately. Refined carbohydrates can be used in situations where there is a great amount of energy being expended at the time of consumption. Long distance runners and tri-athletes have learned to "carbo load" their bodies the evening before a big race. It has been shown that if the carbohydrates are consumed, and the athlete engages in strenuous exercise within a relatively short period of time after consumption, no long-term harm results because they can be burned off quickly.

Let's say, you are on a long hike and are getting tired. If you have a candy bar available, you can turn the energy from the sugars of the candy bar directly into fuel to be consumed by your muscles. It is much more complicated than that because many other factors are involved besides just the fuel being provided; but a candy bar can be used without much damage to the system if a significant amount of energy is being expended immediately.

The greatest degree of harm occurs when the person is not doing anything and consumes refined carbohydrates. When pure fuel enters the body and is not consumed, the body has an innate process for storing that fuel. The body is designed to not waste fuel, or excrete it, unless there is a problem storing fuel in the cells. That problem is called diabetes and one can see sugars in the urine as a result of the body not being able to get the glucose into the cells efficiently.

The process that is natural for the body to use when pure fuel, or sucrose, is consumed and not burned is part of the so-called "citric acid" cycle, or "Krebs" cycle. Sugars that are not needed for fuel are turned into fats. The fats, which are formed by refined sugars, are called triglycerides.

Triglycerides are part of the fat profile you receive when you are tested for cholesterol levels. It has been my belief for years that triglycerides are more harmful than cholesterol. I explain that further in the chapter called "Fats and Fallacies." Some research is now showing my belief may be quite accurate. The reason is triglycerides are the "glue" that binds the cholesterol plaques to the arterial walls.

The body prefers complex carbohydrates as they come in a form which causes the release of the sugars to be more gradual, and they contain co-factors that assist sugar digestion and energy production. Over indulgence in complex carbohydrates can lead to gas production as is the case when you eat too much fruit at one time, or mix sweet and acid fruits, or fruits and proteins.

So, we can see then that complex carbohydrates are generally better for our health. They stress the body less and provide glucose in a more controlled fashion. They are part of the natural design.

Fats

Fats which can be digested are broken up into their building blocks which are used for either building other necessary fats in the body, and/or as a source of energy when needed. The important aspects of fat metabolism are discussed in a later chapter called, "Fats and Fallacies." The body needs usable fats to make hormones, myelin sheathes for nerves and "good" cholesterol to clean the "bad" cholesterol out of the blood stream.

Proteins

Proteins are the most difficult foods to digest. The tightly bound amino acids, which make up the proteins, need enzymes to assist in their digestion. Enzymes are themselves proteins. Enzymes act as "keys" that mechanically start to open the "locks" (chemical bonds) which hold the amino acids together. More in-depth discussion about protein digestion and its consequences is provided later.

pH

Another aspect of digestion that is important and does not get much attention is the pH of digestion. Each of the three types of foods is digested at an optimal pH. Not so surprisingly, the optimal pH for each of the food types is different. Proteins digest best at a very low (highly acidic) pH of 1 to 3. Fats digest best at a moderate pH of approximately 3 to 4.5, and carbohydrates at a relatively high pH of approximately 4.5 to 6. The numbers are not exact and vary with whomever you review, but the concept is accurate. From these numbers, we can see the body is designed to digest one type of food at a time.

Carbohydrates can be broken down in the stomach in a matter of 30 to 45 minutes. Fats will take 1 to 3 hours; and proteins can take up to a full day or longer to be pre-digested before leaving the stomach. What also may be inferred by the digestive times of the various types of food is if you intend to eat a dessert with a meal, it is best to eat the dessert first and then wait 45 minutes for the rest of the dinner. Children will love this.

As we age, the body's ability to produce HCl (hydrochloric acid) in the stomach drops off. Consequently, there may be a need to supplement with Betaine Hydrochloride especially with protein meals.

Mixing Food Types

What happens when you mix the types of foods in any given meal? The body has sensors in the mouth which prepare the stomach for the arrival of the food. Whenever protein is sensed, the acid secreting cells of the stomach go into high production to bring the pH to a level of 1 to 3 to initiate the difficult process of pre-digesting protein. If you add carbo-hydrates, like bread, to the highly acid stomach, the carbohydrates are turned to gas quickly. This explains one of the reasons for gas production when you eat a typical hamburger, fries and a soft drink meal. This is what causes the "bloated" feeling after a Thanksgiving dinner. Refined carbohydrates in the form of pumpkin pie are thrown on top of a large protein meal. Having felt "full" before the dessert, one usually feels "bloated" after dessert.

What has become normal for most Americans eating the Standard American Diet or "S.A.D." is they do not feel as though they are full until they have the "bloated" feeling.

Gas Production

Another reason for gas production is the fact that most foods are not chewed properly to help the process of pre-digestion. Any foods which are not digested will have a tendency to form gas in the intestinal tract. Carbohy-drates tend to ferment; fats become rancid, and proteins putrefy. All of these events produce gas, and the rancid nature of fats and putrefaction of proteins produce foul smelling gas.

Most wives and mothers of boys can attest to the fact that if one consumes too much of any of the food types, especially protein, gas will be noticeable. The process of gas production for animals is similar.

Whenever an animal cannot fully digest the foods consumed, and it remains in the intestinal system, gas will be produced. That is why the large cats, which exist on large quantities of protein, have much shorter intestinal systems than humans. What is not digested is eliminated quickly, so putrefaction does not hinder the animal's ability to function.

Intestinal gases are toxic and the absorption of the foul byproducts can inhibit clear thinking. The difficulty of digesting proteins is also indicated by the fact that large cats nap after filling their stomachs. (As does "Uncle Joe" after a complete Thanksgiving dinner.)

An Owner's Guide

Chapter 4
Candida

A yeast called "candida" thrives on the byproducts of incomplete digestion mentioned in the previous chapter. Candida used to be considered just a vaginal concern for women. What has occurred is that it is now a systemic problem for many Americans. It has even been reported that some individuals with severe cases of candidiasis have gotten drunk after eating pasta. The candida works on the pasta and ferments the undigested portion into alcohol.

Intestinal Bacteria

Almost all individuals who are overweight have a systemic candidiasis problem. People who have been on antibiotic therapy programs almost always suffer the fate of candidiasis, because the antibiotics will destroy the "good" intestinal bacteria, as well as the "bad" bacteria. Acidophilus and bifidus are two forms of beneficial, or "good" bacteria, which are eliminated as a result of antibiotics.

Candidiasis is an epidemic at this time in America. If one has the problem of candidiasis, then a major portion of consumed food may be going to feed the candida. The waste products of the candida are absorbed through the intestinal system making the body extremely toxic.

Sputum Test

A simple test can be performed at home to determine if you have candidiasis. On your nightstand, have a glass of tap water left out overnight. Upon arising in the morning, before you even get out of bed, gather sputum in your mouth and spit it into the glass of water, and allow the sputum and water to sit for at least five minutes. If the sputum disperses all across the top of the water, begins to have "dendrite-like" spicules (thread-like extensions) hanging down into the water, or sinks, then you have candidiasis.

I would suggest you see a health care professional for treatment. The typical medical approach for candidiasis is to eliminate all carbohydrates, including fruits. I have found this approach to be less than ideal. The reasoning behind the elimination of carbohydrates is because candida has been shown to grow on petri dishes in the lab when given sugars. That is true. What is not understood is candida thrives on all byproducts of poor digestion.

My suggestion would be to eliminate the foods which are difficult to digest, or stressful to the body, i.e., heavy proteins, cooked fats, and refined carbs. Eat small amounts of all foods. Do not mix food types, and supplement with betaine hydrochloride, especially with protein meals. (Betaine Hydrochloride is not recommended for people with ulcer or acid reflux problems.) Increase the intake of water before meals and one to two hours after meals. Take digestive enzymes with every food substance. Supplement with certified acidophilus cultures. They will inhibit the growth of candida. The process may take two weeks or longer to be accomplished. You may consider colonic therapy with an inoculation of acidophilus culture as a faster means of accomplishment.

There is a product called "Agrisept-L ®," which I feel is unsurpassed in its effectiveness against candidiasis.   It is distributed by a company called "Essentially Yours Industries." Check the internet for it.

An Owner's Guide

Chapter 5
Overeating

Overeating is also a national epidemic. More than sixty percent of the American population is significantly overweight. Why has this occurred? There are probably as many reasons for overeating as there are people who are overweight. A few of the reasons that come to mind are shared here.

Satisfaction vs. Bloating

The "bloated" feeling mentioned earlier is usually the only indication most people use to tell themselves they are "full." What happens is the body is using its sensors (collectively called the appestat) to tell it when all the nutrients it is looking for have arrived. If we do not have all the nutrients needed to heal and grow, the body gives us a signal it is not "satisfied." Instead of realizing the food we are eating does not have all the nutrients the body needs, we mistakenly interpret the signal as telling us we are still hungry. Consequently, we tend to eat more of the same unsatisfying food in an attempt to become satisfied. You can never eat enough unsatisfying food to become satisfied. The result is overeating until we feel "bloated" and think only the "bloated" feeling means we are "full."

Often the feeling of not being satisfied still exists when we are bloated and we somehow get the feeling we are denying ourselves when we stop eating. Have you ever said, "I am really stuffed, but I still feel hungry."? If so, then you are not eating enough satisfying foods. The foods which are satisfying are

33

typically fruits and vegetables which supply the needed vitamins and minerals.

Food Addictions

Overeating can also be caused by food addictions. Food addictions are often the result of eating foods to which we are allergic, or at least to which we have a sensitivity. Sometimes the food is associated with the feeling of "comfort." These "comfort foods" are connected psychologically to childhood memories. Rewards for good behavior, or special treats when we may have been sick can become psychologically addictive. Chocolate seems to fit that bill for many, many people, including yours truly.

When we feel stressed, mistreated, or misjudged, we can tend to seek "comfort" foods. When the bad feeling does not go away right away, we tend to overeat the "comfort" food.

Self Punishment

Some people choose to overeat food in order to punish themselves. This may come from having a low self-esteem. Many dieters feel they have "failed" when they eat something they thought they should not have eaten, then judge themselves harshly and decide to punish themselves by gorging on foods, primarily "comfort" foods.

What actually may be going on, or may be going on simultaneously, is a subconscious belief that one does not deserve what one really wants. This concept is addressed in one of my seminars called, "Turn

Your Dreams Into Reality." I teach a process, which allows you to find the subconscious belief and eliminate it. (For more information on the seminar see my website at swww.drjimw.com.)

An Owner's Guide

Chapter 6
Why Not Coffee and Cigarettes?

How many people fit the mold of having to have one or two cups of coffee in the morning in order to even think about going to work? Some need cigarettes as well. Why? We all know caffeine and nicotine are addictive, but how do people fall into the "trap" of taking these "drugs of choice?"

Some fall prey to "peer" pressure in elementary or high school. Smoking can play a role in being part of a group, which rebels. Some smoke because their parent(s) smoked. Coffee may follow that same for-mat, especially if one stays out late at night and then has to be functional in the morning.

Breaking the Fast

When awakening in the morning, the body has been without food for eight to twelve hours. That is how the morning meal got its name of "break-fast." The body has fasted for eight to twelve hours and now needs to have the blood sugar level raised in order to function. So the body was designed to "break-the-fast" by eating.

The design model calls for food to raise blood sugar levels high enough to have the brain function. The best foods to accomplish that goal are fruits. If we eat fruits for breakfast, the body quickly digests the fruits and our blood sugar levels rise to the point of being conscious enough to start the day. If we eat only fruits, we are supporting the body's desire to digest only one food type at a time. This provides

37

the least stress to the digestive system and the body in general.

Caffeine and Nicotine

Yet what do the majority of people do for breakfast? They drink coffee. Some drink coffee and smoke a cigarette. Why would someone choose coffee and/or cigarettes? The answer lies in the effect of the drugs: caffeine and nicotine. Both drugs are adrenal stimulants. They cause the adrenal glands, which sit atop the kidneys, to secret hormones, which cause the liver and muscle tissue to release stored glycogen into the blood stream in the form of glucose. The process is called "gluconeogenisis," or, a "new way to make glucose."

Addiction

Any drug, which gives one the feeling of having more energy, just like cocaine, very easily becomes addictive. Caffeine and nicotine are like cocaine in that sense. As the person eats less and less healthy food, the body has less and less energy. It remembers if it consumes some coffee, and/or smokes a cigarette, it has the "feeling" of having more energy. The addiction does not take long for someone who has poor eating habits. Someone may have relatively good eating habits and still feel the "need" for coffee because the body likes a warm drink in the morning. Herbal teas or fresh lemon and water are great substitutes.

Peer pressure in the office for coffee can be as strong as peer pressure to smoke cigarettes for the high school student. I began drinking coffee in the Army because everyone else did it. The morning I awakened and saw my hands shaking, I decided I would never drink coffee again, and have not, for over 25 years.

Coffee Break

If the elevation of the body's blood sugar level is not sufficient, many people find the supplementation of a doughnut will fill the gap, and they then will be able to function. The "coffee break" is a relatively modern habit, developed because people's blood sugar levels rapidly fall and need another "dose" of the sugar "drug" to keep functioning. Doughnut supplementation goes right along with the coffee break, and blood sugar levels will go spiking right back up.

This yo-yoing of the blood sugar level causes a high degree of stress on the pancreas. Long-term abuse of the pancreas, along with poor eating habits, can leave the pancreas less able to do its job and insulin production may decrease as years go by. It would not surprise me if the high incidence of adult onset diabetes was facilitated by the abuse of the pancreas from caffeine and nicotine, combined with poor eating habits.

The Ideal Way to Eat Each Day?

An ideal way to eat each day would have to follow the design for the body. We have already discussed that the body digests each food type at a different optimal pH. So it seems logical to follow that model.

Breakfast

The ideal breakfast is one of all fruits. By that I do not mean "a" banana, or "an" apple. The amount of fruit must be sufficient to sustain the body for at least two hours. Depending on body size, two or more pieces of fruit are necessary to accomplish the goal of functioning without outside stimulation. Fruit will raise the body's blood sugar level quickly.

It is best to eat the fruit, or have the fruit blended, rather than have a large quantity of juice. Juices have a higher concentration of sugars than the fruit itself. If the body is looking to be satisfied, it may have the tendency to want a certain "volume" of food in the stomach. The volume of juice would contain much more sugar than the same volume of fruit and you may wish to dilute the juice 50-50 with water.

The fiber in fruit is an essential aspect of keeping the body cleansed. If someone is sensitive to the level of sugars in juices, he/she may wish to take chromium picolinate and zinc picolinate to assist in sugar metabolism. Severe sensitivity to fruit sugars may indicate an allergy to the fruits, or more seriously an early sign of the propensity for type II diabetes. Hypoglycemia is often a precursor for type II diabetes.

Break Time

After the blood sugar levels spike upward from fruit sugars, the pancreas secrets insulin and the blood sugar levels begin to drop. As we feel we need more energy, the best food at the "coffee break" time is a small handful of raw nuts. (Pecans, walnuts, cashews, macadamias, but not almonds, unless they have been soaked for at least 12 hours. See the section on raw vs. cooked.) Nuts provide fats and proteins, which raise the blood sugar levels more gradually than fruit, and sustain the proper levels longer, because it takes longer to digest the nuts completely.

Lunch

This takes us to lunch. An ideal lunch would be a baked potato and a salad. The complex carbohydrate of the baked potato is again a slower release of the carbo-hydrates. The blood sugar levels will be maintained until late afternoon.

Some people prefer to avoid potatoes due to their blood type, so another quick lunch is one of broccoli "coleslaw" with raw pine nuts, cherry tomatoes and an appropriate salad dressing. The pine nuts are very rich and satisfying.

A salad without a baked potato, pine nuts, or something else that will have some sustainable blood sugar as a result of digestion, may cause a low blood sugar level. Supplement with raw nuts as needed.

The typical lunch of a hamburger, fries and a soft drink, causes a spiking of the blood sugar from the sugars of the soft drink, and then requires the body to spend a great amount of energy attempting to digest the protein of the hamburger, or even chicken breast, if someone thinks that would be healthier. The result is a pooling of blood in the intestinal region to assist in metabolism and digestion of the

41

heavy protein. This pooling of the blood, and the result of the pancreas secreting large quantities of insulin for the sugars, causes what is called "post prandial hypoglycemia," or "low blood sugar after eating."

We feel the low blood sugar level as the inability to stay awake after a typical lunch. (Remember your classes after lunch in high school or college? It was a good time to have a pillow strapped to your forehead, and/or to wear a neck brace to prevent whiplash as your head hit the desk behind you.) (Time for coffee and a cigarette?)

End of Work Day

Near the end of the "normal" workday, let's say 3:30 to 4:30, it is time again for some fruit. A banana or apple may be sufficient unless you are planning to exercise after work. If so, at least two pieces of fruit are needed.

Dinner

Dinnertime is the time for protein. Six to eight ounces of chicken breast, turkey, or fish is best. Raw, or lightly steamed vegetables accompany the protein. This is not the time for a baked potato. The starch of the potato will not digest well with the acid, which is necessary for the protein. Beans and rice are vegetarian substitutions for meat protein. Do not confuse these two as "just" vegetables. Rice and beans add to the protein count of a meal and should be limited when eating meat protein. Part of the problem of gas with beans is the fact that beans are both protein and carbohydrate, which is a poor mix. ("Blazing Saddles" anyone?)

Once again, this is the "ideal" format. If one can stay with this for 75% of the time, he/she would be doing well. Remember, perfection is a goal, not a requirement.

An Owner's Guide

Chapter 7
Raw vs. Cooked

Lysozomes

Within every cell of every living thing are packets of digestive enzymes called lysozomes. These packets of enzymes are there because the Designer of the body knew everything which is alive today would perish at some time. Rather than allow the flesh and bones of animals and humans, the trunks and limbs of trees, and the fibers of other plants to pile up, the Designer was thoughtful enough to re-cycle the material.

When a cell wall is torn or damaged significantly, the enzymes within the lysozomes are released and begin to digest the cell so other plants or animals may utilize the materials for growth and/or repair.

Role of Enzymes

Enzymes are proteins that act as "keys" to unlock the bonds between the building blocks of carbohydrates, fats or proteins. If we had no enzymes at all, the temperature required for the breaking of the bonds between the building blocks would have to be approximately 120 degrees Fahrenheit or higher. Our bodies would literally "cook" themselves trying to digest the foods we eat.

Enzymes can be distorted, or bent when heated above 118 degrees F. As "keys" they fit in a very precise way to assist in breaking down tissue. Because they are heat sensitive, they are less effec-

45

tive when the cells they are in are cooked. Because they are proteins, the twisting or breaking of the enzymes is called "denaturation." Because the cells in which they reside are cooked, any protein cell is also denatured. That means the components of the cell are harder to digest. The metaphor is that both the "lock" and the "key" are damaged, and it will take more time and energy in the form of heat to open the "lock." The body does not produce temperatures above 108 to 110 degrees at the most in severe fevers. Consequently, we can see if enzymes are not functioning properly, the food is not completely digested.

Consequently, raw food proponents tout the benefits of eating raw foods. The drawback is that people are used to, if not addicted to, warm, or hot foods. People usually get tired of cold salads all the time. Is there a compromise? Yes, there is. One way to get the "feeling" of warm or hot foods is to gently warm the food, but keep the temperature below 115 degrees Fahrenheit. Enzymes begin to denature at approximately 118 degrees.

Living Foods

The only way I know of to prepare foods at a temperature below 115 degrees was taught to me by Ed Douglas at the American Living Foods Institute (ALFI). This is done by calibrating an electric skillet by filling the skillet with water to two-thirds full and inserting a candy thermometer. Not all skillets are the same and the better the quality, the more sensitive the thermostat. Take note as to what setting will keep the skillet between 110 and 115 degrees, (usually on the low end of warm) and then mark the thermostat on the skillet accordingly. This factor of warmth is what differentiates "living" foods from "raw" foods.

The truth of the matter is most food served in restaurants arrives at your table at less than 115 degrees, except for boiling hot soups. Many gourmet recipes were developed at ALFI using this warming technique.

Chewing

Another aspect of good digestion, which is often overlooked, is chewing. The enzymes that digest the cells can only be released when the cell wall is crushed and/or torn. Chewing is what gets this accomplished. People who have studied this suggest we chew our food at least 15 to 20 times, or more, before swallowing.

Nuts and Seeds

It was mentioned earlier that raw almonds should be soaked for at least 12 hours before eating. This is also true of Brazil nuts. The reason for the need for soaking is that both of these nuts are the seeds of the tree. All seeds have within them digestive inhibitors. The digestive inhibitors are present in order to promote the probability that some seeds will be consumed whole by an animal. If digestion is inhibited, then the seed has a chance to pass through the animal's intestinal system and be deposited on the ground with a supply of fertilizer. All it needs then is to have rainfall and it can germinate. For the same reason, sunflower seeds and sesame seeds also need to be soaked before eating.

Nuts, such as walnuts, pecans, pistachios, cashews and macadamias can be eaten without soaking. Once again I emphasize the nuts should be raw. Roasting nuts causes the fats in the nuts to be less digestible.

Chapter 8
The Body's Healing Priorities

The body addresses problems on a priority basis. Whatever problem is most life threatening is addressed first. There are two conditions which are of utmost concern to the body, other than massive trauma: 1.) foreign proteins in the blood; and 2.) the pH of the blood getting outside of the normal limits.

Foreign Proteins

All venoms, whether they are from snakes, spiders, wasps, Gila monsters, bees, stingrays, etc. are proteins made up of amino acids. As these venoms are absorbed into the blood stream, the body goes into crisis management. Sometimes the body cannot react fast enough to prevent the venom from causing nerve damage, permanent tissue damage, or even death.

When a person has had a bad diet for a long period of time, the body can only do so much with what it has available. A condition that often results from poor diet is called the "leaky gut syndrome." The intestinal system is designed to allow nutrients to pass through actively and passively, and to retard the absorption of toxins and long chains of amino acids called polypeptides. After years of poor nutrition, the body's ability to heal itself and maintain the proper adherence of the intestinal system cells to each other is diminished.

49

As a result of poor adherence of the cells of the intestinal system to each other, toxins and long chain amino acids are allowed to pass through the "leaky gut." The body now experiences what it perceives as "foreign" proteins in the blood. The innate mechanism to sense foreign proteins does not have the ability to differentiate foreign proteins of venom from the foreign proteins from food. Consequently, when foreign proteins from food pass through the "leaky gut," the alarm is sounded and the adrenal system and immune system are stimulated. (This is also what occurs when the immune systems of organ transplant recipients "reject" the donated organ. This is the reason for immuno-suppression for organ recipients.)

Adrenal Stimulation

The adrenal glands release their corticosteroids, which cause the liver and muscle tissue to release their stored glucose, called glycogen, back into the blood stream. This gives the body energy to fight the battle with the foreign proteins. This process, as mentioned before, is called gluconeogenisis. This is the predominant reason for diet shakes to make the dieter feel as though he/she has more energy. All proteins are stimulants, and massive amounts of protein in the shake give one the feeling the shake is doing some good because of the "energized" feeling.

Immune System

The immune system rallies the "troops" and sends its white blood cells to the area around the "leaky gut." The shape of the foreign proteins are sensed by the lymphocytes, as mentioned earlier, and they tell other white blood cells to use this template and make thousands more just like it to attack the protein. This is the antigen-antibody reaction, and is the start of the allergic reaction.

Foreign Protein Storage

The body must react to foreign proteins because they are acids. If the proteins cannot all be digested or eliminated by the white blood cells, the body will attempt to dilute the acids by retaining water and storing the proteins in areas of the body which have fluid. Some of the fluid-filled areas are the joints. Every joint has what is called "synovial" fluid. This is predominantly water, and also has some nutrients for the joints.

These foreign proteins act as physical irritants in the joints and actually erode the cartilage of the joints. The acid content also can erode the cartilage. This can be the beginning of arthritis.

Arthritis

If someone suffers from arthritis, I suggest they eliminate all animal protein for two weeks and see how good they feel. This will be an indicator of how much protein affects the arthritis. Lots of fruits and veggies, preferably raw, will help the body with its toxic load.

Reintroduction of protein should be done gradually and at a much lower amount. The average person needs no more than 75 to 100 grams of protein per day. That is equivalent to approximately one-half of a chicken breast, or 6 to 8 ounces of fish. At least 64 ounces of water should be consumed as well. This does not mean coffee, tea, lemonade, or soft drinks. This means water. The body absorbs water in the stomach. It absorbs the other drinks later in the system because it considers them food; and some of them, like coffee, tea, and soft drinks are considered toxic and may actually draw water from the body in order to flush them out of the system.

A relatively new product available to the arthritis sufferer comes from Nikken and is called "CM Cream®." This cream has been tested and proven to decrease or eliminate pain from chronic arthritis and increase mobility. The fatty acid esters of the CM Cream® apparently allow the rapid absorption of the product and also aid the cell in repairing itself. Nikken also has a capsule form called "Joint."

pH of the Blood

The pH of the blood is the second of two priorities of the body when it comes to survival. We previously talked about foreign proteins in the blood, and now we address pH. The term "pH" is a chemical term that stands for "potential of Hydrogen" and is a measure of the acidity or alkalinity of a fluid or sub-stance. On the pH scale, 7 is considered to be "neu-tral" while 1 is a measure of complete acidity, and 14 is a measure of complete alkalinity.

pH Range

The body is designed to maintain the pH of the blood between 7.35 and 7.45, which is slightly alkaline.

The body will sacrifice everything in order to maintain that range. If the pH gets outside of that range by 0.05 units in either direction, i.e., below 7.30 or above 7.50, death will ensue in a matter of hours. So you can see how important this pH range is to the body.

Diabetes

Often a person, especially a child, is diagnosed with diabetes because they go into a coma. The victim's pancreas stops insulin production and the cells do not take up the blood sugar, or glucose, which is available. Insulin assists in the uptake of glucose by individual cells. The body senses cells are running out of energy and the automatic reaction is to make more glucose.

The body starts to digest itself in order to get more glucose. As a result of this self-protein digestion, the pH of the blood suffers what is called, "ketoacidosis." Ketones are produced from protein digestion of the person's tissues and blood sugar level skyrockets. Once the pH of the blood falls below the critical level of 7.30, the body protects itself by shutting down all activity and goes into a coma. Treatment for such a crisis is injection directly into the blood stream of sodium bicarbonate.

Acids from Stress

Getting back to the body in general, all forms of stress produce acids. The body is an alkaline machine which produces acids. Part of the acid load comes from incomplete digestion of proteins as was mentioned in the previous section. Sodium bicarbonate is the primary buffering system of the body. Sodium bicarbonate helps reduce the acid level by turning strong acids into weaker acids.

We get "sodium" from our fruits and vegetables, not from sodium chloride (or table salt). The bicarbonate ion is recycled by the kidneys. If our consumption of fruits and vegetables is insufficient to maintain the sodium needed for the buffering system, the body has to look for other alkalizing minerals. The largest quantity of alkalizing mineral in the body is calcium, and the body will sacrifice bones in order to operate a buffering system which is designed to lessen the acid load. Calcium bicarbonate is not as efficient a buffer as sodium bicarbonate, and much more of it is needed to come close to doing the job of sodium bicarbonate.

What is the significance of this? The significance is that too much protein, especially protein which is not digested well, causes a tremendous strain on body systems.

Osteoporosis

The common approach to the loss of calcium is to increase dairy product consumption. This is a fallacy perpetrated on the American people. I will now give you my father's famous "milk" lecture. "Milk is a food for the infant of the species from which it came. In order to digest milk, the body needs an enzyme called 'rennin.' Rennin ceases to be produced by the body after the age of two to three, which is about as old as a child gets and still nurses from his/her mother."

There is no doubt there is a lot of calcium in milk, but it is extremely difficult to get to it. As a result, the heavy protein, which contains calcium called casein, is at best, partially digested. This increases the acid load and further depletes the body's bone calcium, potentially causing osteoporosis.

If sufficient fruits and vegetables are not consumed, a person needs to supplement his/her diet with antioxidants and other nutrients. We cannot keep making the body more and more acidic without paying a price. That price is all too often cancer, heart problems, osteoporosis and/or diabetes. As I have told many of my patients, "You are entitled to have more than one problem at a time and most people do!"

pH and Cancer

It is a well-known medical fact that cancer cannot survive in an alkaline medium. There is no better way to prevent cancer than to work diligently to reduce the acid load of the body. We do that best by eating fruits and vegetables, and supplementing our diet with antioxidants. The best way to lower the acid load is to eat less protein. Even a large person needs only 75 to 100 grams of protein per day. As stated before, that is the equivalent of half of a chicken breast.

An additional beneficial measure is to utilize a water treatment system which can make the water you consume more alkaline. There are small appliance systems, which are plugged in the wall and are quite expensive, and then there is a system marketed by

Nikken, which is called a "Pi-Mag ® Water Treatment System" and uses no electrical energy and offers additional benefits as well. I made a video explaining the physics of the system. You can order the video, called, "Physics of Pi- Water" from my website. www.drjimw.com

Chapter 9
Losing Weight

No book on health would be complete without a chapter on weight loss. Here is what I know and believe. DO NOT EVER EXPECT TO LOSE WEIGHT, AND KEEP THE WEIGHT OFF, WITHOUT CHANGING YOUR EATING HABITS AND INCREASING YOUR EXER-CISING! (PERMANENTLY!)

Now for the particulars.

The Design

The body was designed to survive periods of feast and famine. The ability to store energy in the form of fat was essential for survival. As most animals needed to do in the early years of mankind, humans ate as much as they could when food was plentiful, and built up fat stores. Those who were unable to store sufficient fats did not survive the periods of famine, like winter, or desert crossings. The Design Engineer for the body understood the complexities of digestion and alternative fuel-burning capabilities. Thus humans were gifted with the ability to use car-bohydrate metabolism (primary fuel), or fat and pro-tein metabolism (secondary fuel).

We just saw in the last section how overeating can occur. This is a natural tendency gone awry for a myriad of reasons, not the least of which can be psy-chological.

57

What Methods of Weight Loss are Available?

Eat less and exercise more is the basic form of weight loss. It is very straightforward, simple in design, and difficult to maintain.

Eating in a way that supports the design of the body can work if the body knows what you are doing.

Using high protein shakes, or eating meals of only high protein, and not eating carbohydrates will cause the body to lose weight, but at what cost?

Fasting may cause weight loss, but should not be the reason for fasting. It can also lower the metabolism permanently.

General Concepts

If the body has too much fat in storage, we would like to see the fat "burned" off. We know fat is an alternative fuel for the body. What may not be known by the "lay" person is that fat is never burned alone. Protein is consumed at the same time. The body needs amino acids from proteins to repair and maintain the body.

There are a myriad of diets available to the American consumer. There is the grapefruit diet, Dr. Anthony Weil's diet, the Pritikin diet, the Atkins diet, Weight Watchers ®, Jenny Craig ®, protein shakes, Richard Simmon's card program, etc., etc., etc. And there is fasting.

All diets have their good points. The real question to ask is, "Do any of these diets have a physiological cost to them?" In other words, "By participating in a dietary program, am I causing potential damage to my body?" The answer in most cases is, "Yes." If any of the diets call for a high quantity of protein, there is a physiological cost of making the body more acidic; and we have just read that the body considers acidity to be one of the two most life-threatening situations it can encounter.

Protein Shakes and Fad Diets

The protein shakes and most fad diets call for elimination of carbohydrates from the diet, so the body MUST go into "fat metabolism." High quantities of protein are supple-mented in order to prevent the body from digesting itself to get the amino acids it needs to maintain itself. In the biochemical world, these diets are classified as "protein sparing" fasts.

I can assure you, you will lose weight if you utilize one of these weight loss forms. Two questions come to mind: what happens when you reach your target weight; and, what cost must be paid for being on a high protein diet?

Yo-Yoing

When most people reach their target weight, they simply return to their "old" style of eating. This results in yo-yoing, or rebounding, of the person's weight back to the starting weight, or even higher than the starting weight. This happens for two major reasons. 1.) The old style of eating provided too much refined carbohydrate consumption and the body stored the excess as fat. So, if one returns to the old style without increasing the exercise, fat must be regained. 2.) The body has a means of sensing the percentage of body fat it has acquired. When fat stores are reduced as a result of operating on a fat metabolism, the body will turn anything that can be made into fats, into fat, in order to once again reach what it has considered to be the "required" body fat percentage. Because the percentage had fallen so far below the required level, it will often "add" to the percentage "just in case" there is another shortage. Thus, the person not only gains back the weight he/she lost, but the scales tip a little higher.

Physiological Costs of High Protein Diet

Our society tends to attack all problems by doing battle with the "symptom." When dealing with medications, a person often has to take additional medications to "fight" the "side effects" of the first medication. The fact that there are side effects does not often cause our society to pause and take notice. Our society tends to take side effects as acceptable costs for eliminating symptoms.

"Fighting" fat is no different. There is a potentially serious side effect to consuming large amounts of protein as are found in protein shakes, protein bars, and fad diets. The cost is an increase in the acidity of the body. Most people have not heard of the pH of the blood, much less care about it. They are only concerned about losing weight.

I refer you to the previous section on the pH of the blood for more specific information. Suffice it to say, high acid levels as a result of high protein intake make the body susceptible to premature aging and create an environment which is beneficial to bacterial or fungal infections, and abnormal tissue growth (cancer).

Fasting

Fasting should never be used for the sole purpose of losing weight. Fasts can be beneficial for detoxifying and one must be careful about the degree of self-consumption (wasting, or atrophy) which can occur, indicated by urinary ketone levels. These levels should be checked often if a fast lasts for more than a few days. These ketones are acids and affect the pH of the blood.

Eat Less and Exercise More

Eating less and exercising more is simple, yet few people can maintain this approach due to stresses of life, food addictions, and food allergies. This method takes a lot of discipline. Self-esteem issues play a major role in the success or failure of this dietary program over the long haul.

Exercising (a Part of Every Program)

As stated earlier, no one can lose weight and maintain that loss without increasing his/her exercising. This is usually the biggest reason for people not losing and maintaining their loss. Most people have this image of hours upon hours in the gym, sweating and punishing themselves. That is one way to do it.

Running

Running is a tremendous way to exercise AND it offers unique ways to do damage to your body. People, who have learned to run properly, can do so with minimal risk. People, who have not learned to run properly, do so at their own risk. Besides the obvious ways of damage caused by twisting ankles and falling, which can cause bruising and/or break- ing something; the inability to maintain a proper gait creates a lot of stress on the structure of the body and its internal organs.

When someone begins to tire from running, the first thing that usually happens is the gait of the individ- ual falters. Instead of the four basic stages of the foot action, which are; heel strike, rolling slightly to the outside of the foot, rolling to the ball of the foot, and then propulsion from the great toe, the tired runner usually changes his/her gait to a "jogging" gait. In a jogging gait, the entire weight of the body continuously slams onto the ball of the foot or the entire flat foot. Either way, this is not how the body was designed to propel itself for any length of time.

The normal gait with heel strike, etc., provides a "shock absorbing" effect, which minimizes the stress on the ankles, shins, knees, hips, and pelvis. When one jogs, parts of the body that were not designed to absorb the shock (which can be up to several times the body weight of the individual), must take the punishment. This punishment is delivered to the soft tissue of the joints. (i.e., cartilage, bursas and the ligaments holding the joints in place)

In addition, all of the body's organs are jarred with each pounding foot placement. This can result in intestinal sagging, as well as stress to the heart, liver, kidneys, lungs, etc., and for women, damage to breast tissue.

I never recommend jogging to anyone, even to my brothers and sisters in the Marine Corps who take a tremendous amount of stress to their bodies by all of their other training. My suggestions, however, will most likely not have a significant affect on the traditions of the Marine Corps.

At some point a physical price will be extracted and the damage done is not reversible. It is estimated that it costs 15 times as much to treat a problem than it would to prevent it. The damage shows up as symptoms in the body years after the stress was inflicted.

Structurally, the joints thin, meaning the cartilage, which is intended as a shock absorber, is damaged and cannot regenerate. This is severe arthritis. Just look at some of the athletes who continued to play the sport they loved even after they were injured. Years later they suffer agonizing pain just in standing and walking. Surgical knee replacements have helped in this regard, but one might ask if that is what the Design Engineer intended.

My recommendation for running is to run until you are tired and you feel your gait beginning to change to a jogging gait from the proper heel strike, etc., and then walk at a fast pace until you catch your breath and the ability to run, and then run until you are tired, etc., etc., etc. Your stamina will continue to increase.

Walking

The most natural form of exercise is to walk. I highly recommend it. You can walk at whatever pace you choose. Realize the weight-loss benefits come from getting your heart rate up above your resting level and maintaining that higher level for at least twenty minutes. If you do not increase your heart rate, you will find your weight loss will be minimal, if at all.

If time to walk is even difficult to find, then there is a new product, which can assist you.

CardioStrides ®

Many people find it difficult to find time to go to gyms and/or are embarrassed by being in public while trying to lose the intended weight. Nikken has come out with a revolutionary product called "CardioStrides ®." By looking at them, they appear to be athletic shoes with thick soles. Appearances, however, do not tell the whole story.

CardioStrides ® have been tested and marketed in Japan for some time and have shown the ability to increase a person's metabolic rate (fat burning) by 25% if worn for 30 minutes per day. The shoes have the qualities of supporting the heel and maintaining its proper alignment. Proper heel alignment fosters proper lower-leg alignment, which fosters proper knee alignment, which fosters proper hip alignment, which fosters proper pelvic alignment, which fosters proper spinal alignment, which fosters GOOD HEALTH.

After seeing this new product, I would recommend every Chiropractor offer CardioStrides ® to his/her patients to help those patients hold their adjustments better and longer. (This might even make good business sense for healthcare practitioners across the board.)

In addition, by wearing CardioStrides ® in the office, healthcare practitioners can improve their own health and that of their staffs. It seems to me that a healthy healthcare office provides a good example for their patients.

Severely Overweight, Disabled, or "Lazy"

Some people are confined to wheelchairs, scooters, or bed. Some of us just do not want to go through all the "perceived" hassles of working out in the gym, so we have purchased "home" exercise equipment. These devices usually end up becoming expensive "clothes hangers" or "dust collectors." Even though we are not confined to wheelchairs, scooters, or beds, our approach to exercise is as if we were. Is there anything for the real and imagined disabled person?

The answer is, yes! There is an aerobic exercise program available on video called, "Body Flex." The premise behind the tape is that ANYONE can get an aerobic workout by increasing their oxygen intake and getting their heart rate up. Well, Greer Childers has shown us how to do it with a forced-inhalation-forced-exhalation breathing program, which includes isometric contractions in fat deposited areas that helps burn the fat. "Body Flex" is highly recommended for anyone, especially us "lazy" exercisers.

If one is able, and has the desire to be active in working out, water aerobics is another option. Severely overweight people and people with damaged lower extremity joints may wish to use this form of exercise. By exercising in a pool, the buoyancy factor of the body reduces the stress on the joints, allowing more exercising than would be possible if the person were not in a pool.

Eating in a Way that Supports the Design of the Body

Eating in a way that supports the design of the body is a good way to maintain the body's health. It takes discipline and an understanding of what actually goes on when we are dealing with carbohydrate and fat metabolism. As mentioned earlier, the body's primary fuel is carbohydrates. It prefers this metabolism. Why would the body switch to fat metabolism? The body must switch to fat metabolism whenever there are insufficient amounts of (carbs) available to provide the fuel necessary for the body to do what it is attempting to do.

If you begin the day with fruits, the body has the carbs necessary to get started. Let's say you have just learned about how the body prefers to function and you have some weight you would like to lose. From previous discussions, we know there must have been excess consumption in order to build up the fat stores. How do we now start to lose the fat?

The key is to make certain there is always blood sugar available whenever the body needs to perform work. This is essential when the day begins. Fruit for breakfast provides the carbs necessary for raising the blood sugar level in order for the brain to function.

If you choose to exercise in the morning before you have breakfast, you are choosing to force the body into fat metabolism, because there is insufficient blood sugar available to perform exercise without burning fats. This seems like it is just what we want to do but, in actuality, we have told our body we choose fat metabolism over carbohydrate metabolism. Consequently, the body will make sure our body fat percentage remains at a level that will insure we have energy available in the future. When we return after working out, and have a good breakfast of fruits, the body says thank you very much, now I can use the part of the Krebs cycle that converts carbs into fats to replenish my fat stores. We have defeated our purpose for exercising.

What is a person to do? We have to convince our bodies we will provide it with sufficient carbs to perform the daily functions. The challenging part to this is it will most likely take three weeks or more to convince the body there will be sufficient carbs. Once the body has the "history" of knowing the carbs will be there, it will then allow the body fat percentage to drop and the body's fat stores will be reduced.

What this actually means is, before any exercise, a person must consume the amount of fruits and/or carbs necessary to supply the energy for the complete workout. That may require three to five pieces of fruit before exercising, depending on the exercise program.

Initially, there may actually be some weight gain as the body stores the carbs. After three to four weeks the weight will seem to just start melting away. (Does anyone hear the words "patience," "trust," or "faith?") The weight will stay away only if there is a permanent change in the eating habits.

Dietary Programs, Not "Diets"

Dietary programs are not all designed to have a person lose weight. We tend to think of anything that has the word "diet" in it to mean weight loss. There are programs available, designed to return one to health based on physiological considerations.

Dr. D'Amadeo's work regarding eating for your blood type, is a dietary program which offers some sound practices. Similarly, an ayruvedic approach to eating cooked foods according to your body type, as is espoused by Dr. Deepak Chopra in his health facilities, is a sensible way if you plan to eat most of your food cooked.

A Relatively New Product, Calorad ®

There is a relatively new product on the marketplace, which offers an alternative to the typical dietary struggle. The product is called "Calorad ®" and is distributed by the same company, which distributes Agrisept-L ®, Essentially Yours Industries.

How it Works

Calorad ® contains the building blocks for connective tissue. It is produced in a way that the ingredients are not heated and denatured, so the body can utilize these building blocks with little to no digestive energy expended. They are easily taken up through the intestinal wall.

The body does most of its healing during the first two hours of sleep. If it has the building blocks for repair and reproduction of cells, it will begin those processes. In order for the body to do the repair and/or rebuilding, it needs energy. THIS IS THE KEY. If you have not eaten anything for a period of at least three hours prior to going to sleep, the body will have little immediate foodstuffs for energy. Consequently, it will have to burn the body's fats in order to get the energy. Weight is lost while you sleep!

Original Formulation

The original formulation was designed to help egg ranchers get better production from their hens. One of the industry's problems is hens can become fat, which results in fewer eggs. The original formulation caused the hens to lose their excess fat and egg production returned to optimal levels.

The biochemist then considered his own concerns about his body fat and designed the ingredients for Calorad ® based on his success with hens.

The product does work and I highly recommend it for someone who wants to lose weight. The discipline factor with Calorad ® is to not eat for three hours before going to bed.

Beneficial Side Effects

I have found a beneficial side effect with my chiropractic patients. When taking Calorad ®, my patients were able to maintain and hold their adjustments better and longer. The only possible explanation for this improvement in maintaining an adjustment is the body has the building blocks to repair connective tissue when on Calorad ® and the healing/repair of the ligaments is what holds the vertebrae in place.

Some of my fibromyalgia patients have noticed a marked reduction in their pain symptoms with use of Calorad ®.

My Recommendation

My recommendation would be to use Calorad ® and change your eating habits to best support the way the body was designed. Calorad ® can be used continuously without any deleterious side effects. It can only help the body stabilize and maintain flexibility. Exercising must be a part of any program and I recommend the "Body Flex" program, and/or the Nikken Cardiostrides ®, for their simplicity and effectiveness. Remember, even those confined to wheel-chairs, scooters and bed can use the "Body Flex" program. Everyone can breathe; just increase the amount inhaled and exhaled.

An Owner's Guide

Chapter 10
Fats and Fallacies

There had been a "trend" in dietary recommendation to eliminate all fat from the diet. That has been modified to elimination of "bad" fats. Let's look at the issue.

Eliminating Fats

The fad for some time now has been to recommend eliminating fats from the diet. The present alteration of the fad is to say there are some good fats which can be consumed. What is a "good" fat? The medical model of a good fat is anything which begins as a polyunsaturated fat. On the surface, this sounds very reasonable. Polyunsaturated fats cannot stick together as easily as saturated fats. This is the key to "good" and "bad" cholesterol. The "bad" cholesterol consists of fatty acids which are relatively straight in their physical appearance. Thus they can lie close together like "pick-up-sticks" arranged all parallel to one another. "Good" fats have one or more bends in their physical structure. If you can imagine bending your "pick-up-sticks" and then trying to get them together, you can see they will not pack as tightly as the straight ones.

Unsaturated vs. Saturated Fats

What makes the bends in the "good" fats? The arrangement of the hydrogen ("H") atoms in fats causes them to be straight or bent. Nature makes most of its fats bent. By that I mean, most raw, naturally occurring fats, and all of the "essential" fatty

73

acids, are "unsaturated." "Unsaturated" means there are less "H" atoms in the structure than there could be. When there are less "H" atoms than there could be, the structure can have the "H" atoms on the same side of the carbon chain structure, or on opposite sides. Nature prefers the "H" atoms be on the same side. Now, the "H" atoms on the same side take up a physical "space" and also have a "charge" to them like the poles of a magnet.

We all know that similar charges "repel" one another. The combination of the "space" and "charge" causes the atoms to repel one another and "bend" the carbon chain structure. The biochemical term for this configuration is "cis," fatty acids. "Cis" being of Latin derivation for same side. When the atoms are on the opposite side, the biochemical term is "trans." You can see these terms on some of the food products' nutritional labels.

Effect of Heating Fats

How do the "H" atoms determine what side to locate? As I said before, nature prefers the "H" atoms on the same side. (Presumably, the Chief Engineer on this design project knew something about the effects of fats when they are straight and bent, and decided on the bent ones for better survival potential.) If nature prefers the "H" atoms on the same side, how do they get on the opposite sides? This comes about by heating the fats to high temperatures. Interestingly enough, the biochemical term for this is "denaturation," going contrary to what "nature" intended. Why would someone, or some company, heat the fats to high temperatures? The answer is that Nature's fats spoil and become rancid.

Denatured fats have a longer shelf life. Manufacturers of food products cannot afford to have their products going rancid in the warehouses of the distribution centers. Another factor is the fact people like their fats "clear" and "wholesome" looking. Natural fats, for the most part, do not look clear. Almost all oils need to be heated to above 200 degrees Fahrenheit, and some above 400 degrees to become clear. This process does not cause all the "cis" fatty acids to become "trans" fatty acids, but there is a significant number that do.

How can the manufacturers of oils get away with not telling you about this? The answer is the FDA meets with manufacturers to come up with guidelines for labeling products. They have decided that if the oil, from which the final product is made, "began" with no "trans" fatty acids, then they can say their product does not contain them. (And I bet you didn't know that if Florida orange juice is not "sweet" enough naturally from the oranges, they can legally put refined sugar in the juice without telling you it was added.) "Truth" in labeling is not what it means to most of us.

Is there a simple way to know if a fat is good or bad? Yes. Any "cooked" fat is a bad fat. The cooking process and the "processing" process, heat the fats enough to produce "trans" fatty acids. Almost all "raw" fats are both "cis" and polyunsaturated. The fats, which are naturally saturated, and remain "raw," can be used by the body in its normal process of metabolism.

Role of Fats in the Body

Why can't we get along without fats anyway? Fats are necessary for survival and everyday activity. Essential fatty acids are needed to make: 1.) properly constructed hormones; 2.) the myelin sheaths around our nerves; (Conditions such as fibromyalgia, multiple sclerosis, muscular dystrophy and others, have a component of this de-myelination, or thinning of the myelin sheath.) and, 3.) good cholesterol, which eliminates "bad" fats from our bloodstream.

So what is a person to do? If you are going to eat fats, make as many of them "raw" fats as you can, e.g., avocadoes, and raw nuts. Eliminate cooked fats. Do not worry about cholesterol unless it is from cooked foods. Naturally occurring cholesterol is not harmful if it is not cooked.

The most dangerous cholesterol for the human body, is made by the body, primarily in the liver. This is cholesterol that is made from cooked and denatured fats which are consumed. This is called "conjugated" cholesterol. As it is the liver's job to try to do something with this mess, it creates conjugated cholesterol which is the "bad" form.

Danger of Margarine

Margarine may begin with a relatively good oil, but in order to get it to form sticks and tubs it must be heated to temperatures approaching or exceeding 400 degrees Fahrenheit and have hydrogen gas bubbled through it. It must become "saturated" in order to be a solid, or semi-solid, at room temperature.

It has to become exactly what it was not in order to be a spread. The heating and hydrogen bubbling makes this some of the worst "stuff" you could possibly put into your body. Many of the byproducts of this process are carcinogenic. If you wish to have a fat on your bread, potatoes, etc., the best spread available is "raw" butter. Pasteurization does the same thing other heating processes do, but to a lesser extent. It makes "trans" fatty acids out of some of the "cis" fatty acids.

Anyone experiencing the effects of insufficient essential fatty acids, such as fibromyalgia, PMS, menopausal symptoms, high cholesterol, MS, muscular dystrophy, Alzheimer's, Parkinson's, etc., should consider taking a high quality flax seed oil as a supplement. This oil should be cold-pressed, shipped in a dark container, and kept refrigerated. And that's the truth.

Additional supplementation would consist of taking a high quality balanced "B" vitamin complex. The "B" vitamins are essential in fat metabolism.

An Owner's Guide

Chapter 11
Immune System

A major part of how the body is designed to take care of itself resides in the body's immune system. The immune system is not a "part" of the body like the heart or kidneys. The immune system has many components and is similar to the National Guard in that we only really think about it when there is an emergency and it is called into action. The immune system, like the National Guard, always has someone checking out the terrain for possible threats to the homeland.

There are specialized cells which travel in the blood stream and lymphatic system and look for foreign proteins. When an "invader" is spotted, these special cells (lymphocytes) in essence surround the invader and make a template of the physical structure. This template is like a "wanted poster" in the Post Office. The template is used by the thymus gland to produce specific cells which fit a physical part of the "invader" and then engulf it; taking it out of action so it cannot harm our body.

Antioxidants vs. Free Radicals

The immune system also calls on other "volunteers" to assist it. Antioxidants are used to defeat free radicals which are produced by inhalation, digestion of toxins, and strenuous exercising. These free radicals attack the body's cell walls and cause severe damage. These attacks cause premature aging and other more serious situations even to the level of cancer.

79

If one observes a person who has been a smoker for many years, one can see the effects of premature aging. The toxins in the smoke cause the skin to be treated like a "ham in the smoke house." The outer layer gets hardened. This is called "keratinization." The body attempts to strengthen those cells under attack by depositing calcium and other minerals in the cells to "harden" them to attack. The look and feel is often classified as being "leathery." Sunbathers can get the same result from ultra violet rays damaging the skin.

Keeping Abnormal "Growth" in Check

One of the immune system's responsibilities is to check throughout the body for abnormal growth. If there is a part of the body growing faster than it should, or growing when it should not be growing, the immune system is designed to keep that growth in check. In other words, the immune system is designed to stop cancerous growth within the body. A weakened system cannot do this. A healthy person may never know how many times in his/her life the body defeated cancerous growths.

Autoimmune Conditions

Sometimes the immune system goes awry. It starts to destroy the body's own tissues. This is what an "autoimmune" disease is. Some of the known autoimmune diseases are AIDS, lupus, and rheumatoid arthritis. Some investigators believe other problems may have at least an autoimmune component, including MS, ALS, and psoriasis. One that is seldom believed to be an autoimmune disease, which

I believe should be looked into is type I, or "juvenile" diabetes.

When my eldest son was in kindergarten, he and three other classmates developed type I diabetes three months after a mumps virus went through their class. It is believed some aspect of the physical shape of the mumps virus is similar to the physical shape of part of the islet of Langerhans beta cells, which produce insulin in the pancreas. The immune system would then attack the beta cells and destroy them leaving the person without any means of making insulin.

My son did not have any other symptoms of the mumps because his immune system was very healthy. There is no history of diabetes in either side of our family. The probability of four children in a class of 25 to come down with diabetes at the same time without a common outside initiating factor is astronomical.

Stop Smoking

What is the best way to support the immune system? The best way is to attempt to stay away from toxins or protect yourself from the toxins you are exposed to in your daily life. STOP SMOKING!

If you work in a toxic environment wear all the protective clothing and masks which should be provided by your employer. STOP SMOKING!

Attempt to minimize the ingestion of toxins in the foods you eat, including the foods you eat. There are biologically non-damaging detergents available with which to wash all fruits and vegetables. STOP SMOKING!

Avoid foods heavily loaded with preservatives. The preservatives are toxic. The preservatives prevent the food from "spoiling." Bleached white bread is an example I mentioned earlier. Why was flour bleached? So the insects would not eat it. If an insect will not eat it, you shouldn't eat it. STOP SMOKING!

Vitamin "C"

Besides attempting to prevent exposure to toxins, take supplements to assist the immune system. Antioxidants are primary aids to the immune system. In Southern California where they get to chew their air, everyone should be taking antioxidants every day. There are numerous antioxidants available, the most prolific one being Vitamin "C." The chemical name for Vitamin "C" is ascorbic acid. I would never recommend anyone take ascorbic acid by itself. In nature, Vitamin "C" is always accompanied by other "co-factors," which assist it in its performance of its duties. These co-factors are called "bioflavinoids." These bioflavinoids are also antioxidants. Insist on a Vitamin "C" complex with bioflavinoids, and/or an ester "C".

Glutathione

The body's primary antioxidant is "glutathione." Glutathione is produced within the cells themselves. There are glutathione supplements on the market. They do not significantly increase the body's levels of usable glutathione because the supplements are easily digested into the building blocks of glutathione. Because they are "essential" amino acids (They are needed to make other amino acids.), they are then metabolized into other amino acids. Few, if any, of all three of the building blocks get into the cells to make glutathione.

Glutathione is used by the body in several ways: 1.) It protects cell walls from free radical attack; 2.) It converts fat-soluble toxins into water-soluble molecules in the liver to be eliminated through the kidneys; and 3.) It makes other antioxidants more effective by coming into contact with a free radical-antioxidant complex and re-releasing the antioxidant to do its job again.

I know of only one product available on the market which provides the building blocks for glutathione in such a way they are not metabolized into other amino acids. The product is called "Immuno-cal." It is manufactured in Canada. One can get information on the Internet on the product. There are some indications from Japan that Immuno-cal is very effective with hepatitis "C."

I know if my immune system were severely compromised and I had cancer, or any other autoimmune problem, I would be taking Immuno-cal in addition to whatever other therapies or surgeries my doctor and I had agreed upon.

An Owner's Guide

Chapter 12
How the Body Improves Its Health

Detoxifying

No matter where a person is on the continuum of health... from very healthy to transitioning to the spiritual state, the first thing that must be done to improve the state of health is to eliminate the toxins that have been built up in the body. The very first thing the body will do when given proper nutrients and other health facilitating devices, is to begin eliminating toxins from its systems. As the body begins to do this, stored toxins are re-released into the blood stream to be taken to the liver to be processed and removed. As a result, the person may feel as though he/she is coming down with the flu, feels nervous "tingling" sensations, or experiences headaches.

These "symptoms" may be alarming. However, if the person knows what to expect, he/she can realize these are natural signs of detox. I want to make it perfectly clear though that at no time should anyone detoxify at such a rate so as to experience severe symptoms. What are severe symptoms? They are symptoms which do not allow the person to continue his/her normal activities. If symptoms occur that make a person unable to perform his/her normal functions, a healthcare provider should be contacted.

Minor loss of sleep is not unusual. Feverish chills and shaking are severe enough to have the person see a healthcare provider who knows about detoxification.

Proper Detoxification

The proper way to detoxify is to increase antioxidant intake to help neutralize some of the toxic irritation. Because the liver is involved in any detoxifying it should be supported with vitamins and minerals. Vitamins "A" and "B" complex are essential. There are herbal supplements available as well, which may assist, including "Liver Support" from Nikken.

Eating

I would suggest foods which are either difficult to digest, or add stress to the body, (i.e., meat proteins, cooked fats, and refined carbs) should be minimized. Naturally, my recommendation would be to eat in the way that best supports the body. Please refer to the earlier section.

Water

The requirement for water cannot be overemphasized. It is necessary to dilute the re-released toxins and flush them out of the body. An absolute minimum of one-half gallon of good water should be consumed per day, and preferably a gallon. There are oxygenated waters available which might assist. I recommend the Pi-Mag ® water system offered by Nikken as the best overall product for general water consumption, especially during a detoxification program. The magnetic aspect of this system increases the oxygen-carrying capacity of the water 15 to 20 times over that of tap water. This system was mentioned earlier in the chapter on pH of the blood.

It seems that Nikken keeps coming out with new products, which enhance the body's ability to heal itself. Since beginning this book, I have had to add several remarkable products because of their extraordinary capabilities. This time it is Nikken's "Optimizer." This device is an adjunct to the Pi-Mag system mentioned above. This device "optimizes" the oxygen carrying capacity of the water to a remarkable level.

Personal communication with two individuals whose breathing difficulties were reduced because of the amount of oxygen they were receiving from the water after being treated by the "Optimizer" convinced me to taste the water. My personal reaction to the optimized water was that I could not get enough of it. Every time I am around an "Optimizer" I consume at least a quart of water. My body seems to crave the water.

In regards to the "Optimizer," if you have a reverse osmosis water treatment system, you can utilize the "Optimizer" to great benefit. If you have no water treatment system, my recommendation is to get the Pi-Mag Water Treatment System and the "Optimizer."

The emphasis on water cannot be overdone. Our society has notoriously minimized its water consumption. Coffee, tea, soft drinks, and alcohol are all common substitutes for water. All of them cause dehydration. A twelve-ounce serving of any of the above require 3 twelve-ounce servings of water to counteract the dehydration effects of the original drink!

The timing of water consumption can have an affect on the body as well. It is best to consume two eight-ounce glasses of water upon arising. This is to off-set the effects of not having any water while sleep-ing. One eight-ounce glass of water is best con-sumed one-half hour before meals, and another two-and-one-half hours after meals.

To drink water during meals, causes the water to be treated differently than when it is consumed by itself. It also may cause a person to consume more food than he/she otherwise would if no beverage is consumed with a meal.

When water is consumed on an empty stomach, it is absorbed immediately into the body through the stomach. When consumed with meals, it can dilute the stomach acid needed to digest a meal and is absorbed later in the intestinal system.

Once again, I recommend the Pi-Mag water treat-ment system from Nikken for its overall unique abil-ity to provide the most healthful water for your body.

Sleep

As the body detoxifies, it requires more sleep. The body does most of its healing in the first two hours of sleep and in general can only heal itself when it is resting. If one is constantly under stress, more tox-ins are being added to the system.

Little importance is ever given to mattresses unless one has had difficulties sleeping. My recommendation is to sleep on a firm magnetic mattress. A balanced-magnetic-field mattress can facilitate the resting, healing, sleeping, and detoxifying the body needs in order to improve its health.

Nikken offers the best magnetic mattress I have seen in the marketplace. If a person is highly toxic, he/she may need to go through a two-week detox program before being able to sleep comfortably on the magnetic mattress.

The reason this may be necessary is that the body will immediately begin to detoxify when on the mattress. If a person is too toxic, the toxins in the blood stream may be raised to such a level as to make sleeping uncomfortable. Patience and persistence are necessary in order to get the best results in the program to improve one's health.

Fasting

Fasting is a method of detoxifying at a rapid rate. Consequently, it is important to know what you are doing when fasting. NEVER just decide to fast without either reading a great deal on the subject, or consulting with a healthcare provider who has some knowledge about fasting. Most healthcare providers know little or nothing about fasting and it is easy for them to say you should not do it. Do not allow someone else's ignorance to keep you from doing something which can be beneficial.

There are several key issues regarding fasting. First of all, prepare for a fast. Do not begin a fast after you have consumed a typical steak dinner with all the trimmings, unless you like stomach cramps. Start your preparation by decreasing your heavy protein intake for at least a week and increasing your intake of fresh fruits and vegetables.

The Steps in Fasting

If you have never fasted before, begin with a juice fast and begin fasting slowly. Fast for one day, and then break the fast with salad and fresh vegetables. I recommend carrot juice for any juice fast. It is most likely the best fasting juice available. It is high in antioxidants, especially vitamin "A," which aids the liver in its difficult task. It takes many carrots to make a significant amount of juice (typically 5 lbs. per quart). It is commercially available in many supermarkets and health food stores.

Water must be consumed during all fasts. It is essential for survival and detoxification. On a fast, one gallon or more should be consumed per day. If you take nutritional supplements, continue to take them and add some calcium supplementation. I recommend calcium in the form of calcium hydroxyapatite. It is often called "MCHC" for micro-crystalline hydroxyapatite calcium. The normal daily dose is 1500 or 1600 mgs./day. When fasting or exercising heavily, the daily dose can be taken two or three times per day. Calcium will be needed to help prevent cramping. It will almost always come in a combination with magnesium, boron and vitamin "D" so they all are balanced.

Some healthcare practitioners warn against taking too much calcium because of the possibility of kidney stones. This can occur if one is taking a form of calcium which is not very well utilized by the body. Consuming large quantities of calcium carbonate could be a problem. (Calcium carbonate is the form of calcium in stalactites and stalagmites found in caves. It is also the form which clogs old water pipes. Most water is acidic and causes this form to precipitate out on the walls of the pipe, the shower stalls, and swimming pools.) The body has to do something with this virtually unusable form and it will attempt to eliminate it through the kidneys. In an extremely acid environment, i.e., the body of a toxic individual, the alkaline minerals in a "carbonate" form will precipitate out and begin to form stones, just as it does in old water pipes.

After the first day of carrot juice fasting, at least two days should pass before you fast again. As before, no heavy protein, cooked fats, or refined carbs should be consumed.

You may now decide to fast for up to three days on carrot juice. Do not feel as though you have to fast for three days. Listen to what your body tells you. If you feel dizzy, extremely weak, and/or have severe cramping or pains, STOP the fast. You may choose to break the fast for two or more days before beginning again. Do not look at this as a "failure." Just realize your body is quite toxic and cannot handle the rapid re-release of toxins. You get no "gold star" or "extra points" for punishing yourself.

Once you have successfully fasted for three days, break the fast as before with salads and vegetables, but this time for a week. You may choose to repeat the three day fast a week later.

91

Once you have successfully completed at least two three-day fasts, you may consider a week-long juice fast. And once you have completed a week-long juice fast, you may consider a water fast. I would recommend the Nikken Pi-Mag water system. If you do not have such a system, I recommend distilled water for the fast. Many people consider distilled water to be "dead" water. To a certain extent this is true. Distilled water is also like an empty sponge. It is able to absorb more toxins than regular water. Distilled water is my "second" choice.

Ketones

When fasting on water, NEVER ALLOW YOUR KETONES TO RISE ABOVE A "TRACE!" (You can get "ketone" sticks from any pharmacy.) More than a trace and your body is consuming itself at too rapid a rate.

After completing a fast, reintroduce foods gently and slowly. Salads, fruits and vegetables will ease the body back into food digestion less stressfully than a hamburger and fries.

Stress Reduction

Most of us in our society live a relatively fast-paced life. Moms have to be "Superwoman" and, if you look at most TV commercials these days, Dads must be brain dead, or otherwise incapable of functioning as knowledgeable, caring human beings. Whatever the level of stress for each of us, there is a simple method of reducing that stress, at least temporarily.

Biofeedback

In the mid-to-late seventies, biofeedback machines were just coming into acceptance. The meters on the machines were all analogue, meaning a deflecting needle gave you your readings rather than a digital readout like most meters now. A physiology professor had a biofeedback machine and was demonstrating it in class. We were learning about the various brain-wave frequencies. The professor had a student volunteer on the machine and had informed us that it was difficult to keep the needle of the meter in the "alpha" range. (The alpha range is that frequency range where rapid eye movement and dream state of sleep occur.) As the student attempted to rest, the needle bounced back and forth only occasionally getting into the alpha range for the briefest period of time.

I then asked if the professor had ever tested someone who was meditating. He said he had not, and asked to test me while I was meditating. When I reached the meditative state, the needle moved into the alpha range and did not move out of that range. This was a clear indication meditation had a very positive physiological effect on the body.

Intuitive Insight

That afternoon after classes, a friend and I asked the professor if we could perform a little experiment with his machine. He agreed. I had had an intuitive thought about this alpha state. I had my friend lie down on his back and I attached the electrodes. I then told him to roll his eyes up as if he were looking at a spot in the middle of his forehead. As soon as he did this, the needle moved into the alpha range and stayed there.

We had intuitively discovered a way to mechanically get the brain in the alpha state. Since then, I have instructed people in doing this during stressful times when they have only a few seconds in which to relax.

I taught high school basketball players how to use this in the last quarter of a game when they needed to make pressure free throws.

I have used it when stuck in traffic. You can do this when you are aware of your energies rising toward anger. This is not suppression. It is a mechanical means of giving yourself time to make a choice about becoming angry, without adding the stress of suppressing that anger.

This technique may be used before each golf shot, tennis serve, pitched baseball (whether throwing or hitting), big meeting, or when you want to talk with your children about serious matters. You may choose to try it now. Before you begin, get a sense of the degree of tension, which exists in your shoulders right now. Now roll your eyes up and take two deep breaths. If there is discomfort in the eyes, lower them slightly until the discomfort is gone. Once again get a sense of the tension in your shoulders.

I use this method when I consult with individuals or corporations in reducing conflict and tension. It is an effective technique to lower stress in personal situations and/or corporate environments.

Physiological Effects of Stress

Here are just some of the physiological effects on the body caused by stress.

1.) The arteries are narrowed causing the heart to pump harder; otherwise known as high blood pressure.

2.) Vision is narrowed causing you to lose some of the peripheral aspects of vision. You may not see something that could harm you or someone you love.

3.) The heart rate is increased causing a potential overload on the heart, which is a muscle and can be fatigued and damaged.

4.) Thinking is not as clear and judgment is impaired because the body is in a state of "fight-or-flight" survival.

5.) The adrenal glands are stimulated and if this is a frequent state, the adrenal glands may be overused leading to fatigue or collapse. This can affect the body's ability to fight off bacterial or viral infections and possibly some cancers.

6.) The muscles are in a constant state of tension, causing production of oxyradicals, which are damaging to your cells and toxic to your liver.

7.) Digestion is impeded, causing intestinal problems, ulcers, and further toxicity.

8.)The frequency of vibration of the person is lowered, causing others to feel uncomfortable around him/her.

Retracing

As the body begins to heal itself, it will often experience something called "retracing." Retracing is best explained as re-experiencing a milder form of symptoms which were experienced as the person got to the place he/she is. For example, if one has had difficulty breathing as a symptom earlier in life, then similar, but usually milder symptoms of difficult breathing may be experienced for a short period of time on the way back to health.

The discomforts of retracing can be minimized by drinking great quantities of water and supplementing with anti-oxidants

How to Measure Your Health.

pH

A physical measurement of the pH of one's saliva and urine will give a fairly accurate idea of the biochemical state of the body. We live and die at the cellular level and the level of acidity, or pH, is a good indicator as to how healthy our cells are.

My recommendation for those interested in finding out about their relative health is to get the book, "pH, Your Potential For Health" written by Dr. M. Ted Morter, Jr., M.S., D.C., and follow the guidelines given by Dr. Morter. His book is available through Morter Health Systems, (800) 443-2378 and on my website at www.drjimw.com.

Detoxifying the Skin

As stated above, we live and die at the cellular level and the level of acidity, or pH, is a good indicator as to how healthy our cells are. The skin is a perfect example of this. Our internal pH is optimized between 7.35 and 7.45. Our external, or skin, pH is optimized between 5.5 and 6.5, which is acidic. You can go to any pharmacy and get pH paper or test strips. Just moisten some of the paper and allow it to adhere to your skin for a few seconds. You will see the paper turn the color indicating a pH of between 5.5 and 6.5. When washing, especially your face, it is best to use a cleansing product that has a similar pH. Nikken's Swiss Soflower products pro-vide the balanced pH.

Many expensive bars and liquids have a pH of 11 or higher which is very alkaline. Such cleansers will cause a damaging, drying effect on the skin.

Besides the regular cleansing, toning and lotion products, Nikken now has exclusive ThalassoKea products, which have won awards around the world. I tried an eye patch on one eye for twenty minutes. The difference between the bags under my treated eye vs. the other eye was remarkable.

An Owner's Guide

Chapter 13
Alternative Therapies

Chiropractic

Techniques

Because the body has a skeletal structure, chiro-practors were invented. The generalized concept of chiropractic is everything in the body is controlled either directly, or indirectly, by the various nervous systems of the body. I am not certain how many "official" techniques there are in chiropractic, but suffice it to say there are at least 13 of them. Actually, I know very few chiropractors who practice a "pure" technique. Most all chiropractors use what they have found to be effective for them from all the techniques they have tried or encountered, and use that assimilated technique with their patients. Not all techniques use a manipulative force and not all manipulative force is delivered manually, some use "tools" or "devices." The non-force techniques can utilize energy balancing methods to improve the ability of the body to heal itself.

For someone who is thinking about going to a chiro-practor for the first time, my advice is to go to one and see how you feel as a result. If one technique is not successful for you, try another. Do not ever feel, because you saw one, two, or even three chiroprac-tors, you have tried all of chiropractic.

Why see a Chiropractor?

Why should you consider a chiropractor? The Designer engineered the body to take care of itself, as long as it is given the right building blocks for growth, energy, and repair. Because the body has ten times the number of sensory nerves coming from the various parts of the body, the computer control system, i.e., the brain, is designed to receive damage reports due to falls, accidents, unhealthy food, etc., and give directions to the "peripherals" to take care of repairs. If the communication system of the body, the nervous system, is compromised in any way, the communication is incomplete or faulty. Incomplete or faulty communication hinders proper repair.

The communication system can be compromised most easily as it exits its bony covering, the spine. As misalignments of the vertebrae of the spine, or "subluxations" occur, the ligaments of the spine are stretched and/or torn. This brings about a reflex reaction to put the small muscles of the spine in that area into a "splinting" spasm in order to hold the vertebrae as well as possible.

In addition, swelling occurs. The combination of spasm and swelling can easily put pressure on the nerves coming out between the vertebrae. The "old" descriptive expression was that it was like "pinching a hose." This phrase is not accurate from an anatomical perspective.

What actually occurs is a very small nerve, called the recurrent meningeal nerve, is compromised. This nerve re-enters the spinal cord and communicates

100

with nerves as far away as three vertebral levels above and below the site of misalignment. This aberrant nervous communication can cause muscles and organs innervated by the nerves from all of those vertebral levels to be affected.

By correcting the misalignment, the pressure on the recurrent meningeal nerve is reduced and/or eliminated; thereby allowing proper communication between the "computer" and its "peripherals."

What has not occurred is the total healing of the stretched and/or torn ligaments. It is the job of the ligaments to hold the bones of the body in place. If the ligaments are stretched and/or torn, healing is needed. Ligaments receive very little blood supply, consequently, they do not heal rapidly. If they are not healed completely, it is easy for the vertebrae to misalign again. This is the reason chiropractors need to see their patients regularly after an injury. The more frequently the vertebrae are realigned, the better chance the body has to heal the ligaments and maintain the integrity and flexibility of the spine. It is not as simple as stitching up a cut and coming back a week later to take the stitches out.

Optimal use of Chiropractic

Most people have heard of going to see a chiropractor when they have "back" problems or headaches. The optimal use of chiropractic care is to stabilize the spine, have the maximum flexibility possible and then maintain it. Many other conditions of the body can be helped by visiting a chiropractor, because the body will then be able to take care of itself.

Most chiropractors have helped with health challenges that did not respond to typical "medical" care. My admonition to my students while teaching at Logan College of Chiropractic was if they did not perform what would be considered to be a "medical miracle" within the first four months of practice, they should get out of chiropractic.

Chiropractic and Heart Attacks

My own story is a point in case for treating the spine and having an affect on areas of the body other than just the spine, or, in other words, a "medical miracle." While in the Army and stationed at Edgewood Arsenal, MD, I took a severe fall in a rainstorm and felt problems throughout my back and neck. I went to a local chiropractor and he was able to realign some of the areas of my spine, but the upper back and lower neck were rigidly misaligned and not responding to treatment.

Over a period of the next ten days, I began developing crushing chest pains, or "angina." The anginal pains increased in frequency and intensity during that period of time. When the pains felt as though an elephant were standing on my chest and lasted for over 2 and 1/2 hours, I decided I needed to do something about it. A friend took me to the emergency room of the Army hospital at Aberdeen Proving Ground. My personal belief was that I had a blood clot moving around and it had gotten to my lungs. When they ran an EKG on me, the technician told me I was having a heart attack.

At this time in my life, I was in the best physical condition I had ever been in, including while at West

Point. Two weeks prior to the fall, I had come in second in the post handball tournament, played on two softball teams and golfed at least two times per week. I was 6'7" and weighed 215 pounds. I was a lean, mean, health-conscious machine. (Well, almost, an occasional hot dog and beer were had.)

My former wife informed my parents who arrived at the hospital the next day. While in the intensive care ward, I had developed an arrhythmia and had an artificial pacemaker snaked through a vein in my right arm and into my heart.

When I saw my father, I told him my back was as painful as the anginal pains. He managed to adjust my upper back while in a soft bed and with all the paraphernalia attached to my body in the form of pacemakers and monitors of various kinds.

When he adjusted me, it was not 30 seconds later, or 10 seconds later; my anginal pains were relieved IMMEDIATELY, as well as my back pains even though no one knew or expected the anginal pains would be affected at all by the adjusting.

It was as if someone turned off a light switch. I lay in bed absolutely stunned by the immediacy of the benefit of the treatment. It was because of this experience I decided to accept medical retirement from the Army and pursue a chiropractic education. In the twenty plus years I have been licensed, I have had the good fortune to be able to stop three heart attacks in progress.

So, if anyone asks me what chiropractic can do besides take care of backaches and headaches, I have a good story to tell them. (This is not to say when experiencing heart attack symptoms, one should not go to the emergency room. Go there, and see the chiropractor later. If you are a chiropractor, and a friend or patient is experiencing such symptoms, there is something you can do to help by adjusting the first ribs.)

Use of Orthotics

Many chiropractors, myself included, offer orthotics to their patients. Orthotics are devices placed into shoes to help align the bones of the feet and ankle. This alignment proceeds up the skeletal structure through the ankles, knees, hips, pelvis, and spine. As stated earlier with the CardioStrides® and the support they give to the body while walking, this alignment helps the body maintain health. If someone suffers from severely fallen arches, or other foot instability problems, he/she may need orthotics even in the CardioStrides® to feel comfortable and stabilized.

Orthotics can be worn in most shoes, and provide the best support when used with athletic shoes or other shoes with laces. There are several forms of orthotics available on the market and offered from healthcare providers.

I recommend soft, pliable orthotics made from impressions of the feet, rather than non-weight-bearing casted or off-the-shelf varieties. The type made from standing, full-foot impressions will usually provide support for the transverse arch, as well as the well-known longitudinal arch.

The transverse arch can "fall" like the longitudinal arch. When this occurs, "hammer toes," "dropped" metatarsal heads, or other painful problems may result.

The orthotics I use and recommend are from "Foot Levelers, Inc." The easy-to-use, crushable-foam impression kits make taking impressions very easy. They can be mailed to the person needing orthotics and he/she can make the impressions themselves, and then send the kit back to the healthcare professional.

Some orthotics are made of hard plastic. I have seen people who have used these expensive forms of orthotics develop a weakening of the muscles of the anterior part of the lower leg. Often, this form of orthotic does not address the transverse arch either. The hard orthotics do not allow the foot to go through all four phases of foot action necessary for proper foot dynamics. The soft orthotics allow for all four phases to occur.

As stated earlier, alignment and balancing of the entire body with use of proper orthotics can affect things far removed from the feet. I have seen people with headaches no longer have headaches as a result of aligning and balancing the feet, which are the foundation of the body when one is upright.

Impression kits may be ordered from my website at www.drjimw.com. The orthotics range in price from $150 to $250, depending on the need. There are even orthotics for men's and women's loafers and women's heels up to 2 inches.

Massage Therapy

Most people consider massage therapy a frivolous indulgence of the wealthy. It is my belief the best treatment someone can get is a good chiropractic adjustment followed immediately by a thorough full-body massage. There are many forms of massage available including shiatsu, Swedish, trigger point therapy, bodywork, deep tissue, and many, many more. One of the purposes of massage therapy is to assist the body in removing toxins and thereby relaxing muscles. If the body has spinal misalignments, and they are not corrected, then the benefit of the massage will be lessened because the affected nerves will cause the muscles to go back into spasm shortly after the massage.

The reason some forms of massage feel uncomfortable while experiencing them is because of the release of the toxins in the muscles from being in spasm or from overwork. Lactic acid and other toxins tend to build up in certain areas of the musculature where the nerves actually connect to the muscles. These points have been called "trigger" points. These points are also treated with muscle stimulation devices.

During massage, toxins are physically forced from the area and because they are acids they cause the nerves to feel a "burning" sensation. My suggestion is to take as deep a massage as you can tolerate. Realize your tolerance will increase with the frequency of massage because there will be fewer toxins remaining. Antioxidants and copious amounts of water are needed whenever you have a good massage.

Craniosacral Therapy

I choose to mention "Craniosacral" therapy in this section because it is most often associated with massage therapists. This therapy primarily focuses on balancing the energies of the body and can have a beneficial effect for many deep-seated conditions not necessarily limited to muscle tightness. If asked to describe what craniosacral therapy does, I could not specifically do so; BUT the results (from personal experience) are phenomenal.

If someone is not getting any response from traditional healthcare providers, including chiropractors, I highly suggest he/she attempt to find a craniosacral therapist.

Acupuncture

This ancient form of energy balancing is not very well understood by most Westerners. I have studied acupuncture a little and have used it as a modality in my practice for a few years. I understood my limitations and eventually chose to send my patients whom I thought needed acupuncture to practitioners who were more proficient than I.

The theory of acupuncture, as my limited knowledge allows me to state, is the life force energy of the body, called "chi," flows around and through the body following certain channels called "meridians." When the flow of energy is somehow interfered with, there results one or more meridians with excess energy, which is blocked, and their successor meridians with deficient energy. The "needles," which are

actually called "wires," are placed in specific loca-
tions on the affected meridians and other associated
meridians depending on the symptoms of the
patient, or according to a five-element analysis done
by the practitioner. This causes the blockage to be
removed and the energy to flow properly. When
energy flows properly, symptoms are relieved and
health prevails.

My recommendation with alternative healthcare
methods, is to remain open to the possibility that
any, or all, may be needed to help the body do what
it is designed to do, i.e., heal itself. When it comes
to acupuncture, do not hesitate to try it.

If a person's symptoms occur at a certain time every
day, then I recommend using acupuncture first. I
make this recommendation because the "chi" flows
with time, and each meridian pair has a two-hour
period of time when it is supposed to be high in
energy and a two-hour period when it is supposed to
be low in energy. The time of day therefore can
affect the exacerbation or abatement of symptoms.
Many acupuncturists are also herbalists.

Homeopathy

Homeopathy is another lesser-known alternative
health-care modality. Realize I said "lesser-known"
and not of lesser value. The theory behind homeopathy is also an energy balancing methodology. The
understanding of "how" homeopathy works is best
described by using quantum mechanics and I am
sure everyone understands quantum mechanics.
Riiiiight!!!!

If everything is energy and energy cannot be destroyed, as the laws of physics tell us, then even the slightest "ghost" or hint of a frequency of energy persists long after it appears to be gone. Quantum mechanically, what occurs is there is a vibrational energy transfer from the treatment molecules in large concentrations, to the successive dilutions. After all the dilutions have been accomplished it appears that there are no treatment molecules available in the solution   In fact, the frequency is maintained. It is the retained frequency, which is therapeutic.

Naturopathy

Naturopathy is treating the patient with herbs, essential oils, and other food items in a natural way. It also is an energy balancing modality. I would recommend a naturopath over a nutritionist in general terms because a naturopath will have a better understanding of the energies of the body, how they are affected by the various herbs, and explore cause rather than simply treating symptoms.

Magnetic Therapy

We, as Westerners believe magnetic therapy is something "new" and as such seem to have a certain **"arrogance of ignorance"** about us. Magnets have been used for millennia. We are just becoming reacquainted with the use of magnetic energy.

My background in engineering, physics, biophysics, and physiology provides me with a rather unique perspective on magnets, their effectiveness, and their use.

The ancients used "lodestones" in therapy. (Lodestones are rocks from volcanic flow, which have iron molecules in them. While the rock is molten, the iron molecules are aligned to the magnetic field of the earth. The rock cools and solidifies with the iron molecules permanently oriented with the earth's magnetic field. Thus, they have positive and negative poles.) The ancients became aware the negative pole seemed to be soothing and the positive pole seemed to be stimulatory. Consequently, the tradition has been to use the negative pole of the magnet for therapy. What was not available to the ancients was the use of a balanced magnetic field, i.e., both positive and negative at the same time. This was almost certainly not physically possible because the negative and positive poles of the lodestones would attract each other and be physically "neutralized."

Modern technology allows manufacturers to magnetize material in such a way as to situate negative and positive poles next to each other. This creates a "balanced" magnetic field. I recommend balanced field magnets for use. Everything in nature wants to be balanced and the human body is no different.

I recommend balanced field magnets with a Gauss, or "field strength" of 1,000 or less, and no more than 2,000 for emergency use until the pain has subsided. Imbalanced and/or high Gauss magnets will affect the body's electromagnetic field in a way no one can predict, other than certainly putting it out of balance.

Bio-Energetic Synchronization Technique (BEST), developed by Dr. M. Ted Morter, Jr., D.C. demonstrates the body's natural healthy state is with a balanced magnetic field (see next section) and how an imbalanced field affects its symptomatology. By balancing the body's magnetic field, a practitioner enhances the capability of the body to do what it is designed to do, i.e., heal itself.

Magnets Must Work

Because of the laws of physics, magnets must do what they must do. If magnets work for Betty they must work for Bob. Unfortunately, medical scientists feel there is a need for "double-blind" studies to "prove" the efficacy of using magnetic therapy.

No one, not even the top medical scientists in the world, can perform a "double-blind" study on the laws of physics. The laws of physics are "immutable," which means whether you know about the laws or not, or whether you believe the laws or not, you are still subject to them.

Few physical scientists have studied physiology; consequently, they are not familiar with what occurs naturally as a result of injury and/or disease.

I happen to have been trained in both areas and can speak both languages, including "double-blind." If you would like to learn more about how and why magnets work, you can order the video called, "The Mysteries of Magnetics" from my website, www.drjimw.com. The video explains what must happen when magnets are used. It also explains what the "double-blind" studies are really showing. If a person does not respond to magnetic therapy, as the video explains in more depth, it is because the person does not have sufficient antioxidants in his/her system to counteract the acids produced by the injury/disease.

I recommend Nikken magnetic products because of their balanced field and safe Gauss levels.

Palm-Mag ®

While in the process of editing this book, Nikken developed a new method of applying a magnetic field to the human body that is hand operated and affordable. Nikken calls the new item the Palm-Mag ®.

The Palm-Mag® has a spinning magnet which rotates at approximately 23 revolutions per second on one axis, and then rotates that axis. The spinning magnet produces a magnetic energy "plane" that then sweeps through the entire body.

The effects have been rather remarkable, from an anecdotal point of view. There are reports of a man who was due to have bi-lateral amputation of part or all of his lower extremities. After using the Palm-Mag ® 10 minutes at a time, three times per day, for two weeks, his amputation was no longer necessary and his pain from World War II wounds was eliminated.

Upon hearing about this, I used my contacts in Nikken to look at this device. My fiancée had been in an auto accident eight years ago and had had her shin jammed into the dashboard of her car. There was, in essence, a "bone bruise" ever since the accident. The lump, which was the result of swelling of the outer layer of bone called the periosteum, was extremely sensitive to touch. We turned the device on and set it on the wooden kitchen table of the people who had the device. While we were talking about health in general for approximately 20 minutes, the extreme tenderness was totally gone. The lump was gone in two days with no more treatment applied. The tenderness has not returned since, and that has been over eight months.

While presenting a program to a group of Nikken Wellness Consultants and sharing how and why magnets must work, I turned on a Palm-Mag ® the meeting coordinator had received and was explaining what I believed to be occurring with the device. I asked for other anecdotal reports from the audience of the people who had received their Palm-Mag ® early. One of the hands raised was that of a young woman who had never seen the device before. She stated that she arrived at the meeting with stuffy sinuses. She was sitting approximately four feet from me when I turned it on. She said that she instantly felt her sinuses open as soon as I turned the device on.

After reviewing a conversation I had with Klaus Kronenburg, Ph.D., retired chairman of the Dept. of Biophysics at Cal Poly Pomona, it became aware to me what might be occurring with this device. Dr. Kronenburg and his department were charged with determining what was occurring with municipal magnetic water treatment systems and the removal of mineral plaque from the inside of hot water heaters, from swimming pools and shower doors. The only feasible explanation he and his department were able to arrive at was a quantum mechanical one. (Realize that quantum mechanical activities are not subject to double-blind studies because of what is called the "Heizenburg Uncertainty Principle.") Dr. Kronenburg stated that he believed the electrons of the minerals of the water, as well as the water itself, passing through the magnetic field received a "spin" (were energized) to a higher energy level. At this level they were more "biologically active." When the energized calcium molecule let's say came in contact with another calcium molecule precipitated on the side of the pool, or shower door, or water heater, it caused the precipitated molecule to begin to vibrate at the new level making it more biologically active. As such, the precipitated molecule was removed from the pool, door, or heater and returned to suspension.

This quantum mechanical spin on the electrons of molecules can be accomplished by having the magnetic field moving as it is with the Palm-Mag ®. The result of such activity is the enhancement of the body's ability to do what it was designed to do, i.e., heal itself.

No one can completely describe what is happening, and it is not my intention to make any medical claims for the Palm-Mag ®. The only definitive thing I can say is that bodies in the vicinity of the device are seeing marked improvement in their states of health and resolution of some chronic problems, which were previously non-responsive.

I am not a Nikken Wellness Consultant so please do not attempt to order this device from me. If you do not know a Nikken Wellness consultant, contact the company, at www. Nikken.com, to be referred to one in your area.

Hot and Cold Therapy

There is often confusion regarding when to use heat or cold. The simplest indication for either heat or cold is the following. Sharp, stabbing sensations usually indicate localized swelling putting pressure on nerves. To reduce the swelling, use cold. Aching, stiff sensations usually indicate the need for moist heat.

Electric heating pads are not recommended. They usually draw moisture from the body and the electric current can possibly alter the body's electromagnetic field.

There are numerous devices for heating and the method I feel is most beneficial regarding both moisture and the duration of maintaining heat is a product I was recently introduced to called, "Therma-Flax.®" This product will maintain its temperature for up to one hour.

Therma-Flax may also be used for cold therapy. It does not get as cold as ice, but it maintains its temperature for a much longer period, which adds to its therapeutic affect.

Therma-Flax pads may be ordered from my website at www.drjimw.com.

An inexpensive, reusable cold pack is a one-pound package of petite frozen peas. Place a thin dish-

towel between the package and your skin to prevent "burning."

If you have sharp pain and muscle spasms, cold
therapy must be applied long enough to get the
area numb. If you stop the therapy before it is
numb, all you have done is gotten cold. Only when
the nerve endings are numbed will the muscles be
allowed to relax. The relaxation of the muscles
decreases the pressure on the nerves and thereby
reduces the pain.

If alternating heat and cold are recommended,
begin and end with cold. Ice for 20 minutes and
heat for 10minutes. You may wish to use a Jacuzzi
or sauna, but ice before and after the heat.

Why not use heat for acute pain? Heat is soothing
and feels good. What heat also does is it draws
more fluids to the area being heated. The result is
increased pressure from the additional fluids, which
in turn will often cause the pain to be the same or
worse within 15 to 20 minutes after taking away
the heat.

Chapter 14
The Body's Electro-Magnetic Field

In the introduction I mentioned another means of sensing which the body has that is not usually spoken about, or believed, by the majority of the medical establishment. That sensing "device" or "organ" is the body's electro-magnetic field, otherwise called the "aura"."

Why Must There be an Aura?

For those who "poo-poo" the concept of an aura as some "new-age poppy cock," I would like you to know the laws of physics require any living thing to have an aura. The first law of electro-magnetism, sometimes called the "right hand rule," states that if an electron or other charged particle is moving, it generates a magnetic field.

A simple description of a chemical reaction is an exchange, or movement, of electrons, or other charged particles called ions, between atoms or molecules. If one considers the trillions upon trillions of chemical reactions which occur in any living entity each moment of its existence, it can easily be seen that there are trillions upon trillions of electrons moving. Consequently, a magnetic field must exist. Add to this the flow of electrical impulses along all the nerves of the body, and then add the energy flowing along the acupuncture meridians, the laws of physics require there be an electromagnetic field around all living things

The easiest way to describe one of the uses of the aura as a sensing organ is to ask anyone to remember when they may have met someone for the first time and had an immediate "sensation" of either immense attraction, or repulsion. What was going on from the standpoint of the laws of physics? Everything is energy including us. Energy has several properties, the most important of which for our discussion are: frequency of vibration and intensity.

Frequencies can be resonant or dissonant. When there is resonance, the "sensation" is one of immense attraction. When there is dissonance, the "sensation" is one of immense repulsion. So, if you sensed you might have met a "soulmate," or "the devil incarnate," realize it was the interaction of your aura with that of the other person. Some would call it "intuition." Your aura is part of what you perceive as your intuition. When something doesn't "feel" right, there is a physical reason. The energy of whatever, or whoever doesn't "feel" right is dissonant with your energy and is "sensed" by your aura. (And no, you cannot do a "double-blind" study on quantum mechanical effects.)

I am certain this is not the limit of how the body's electro-magnetic field assists, interacts, guides, directs, or otherwise has an affect with, and on, the body and being. My knowledge is limited in comparison to the innate knowledge of the living being.

Intensity and Charisma

The intensity of the aura is dependent upon many factors but can be sensed by other beings. Someone who is considered to be "charismatic" has a high

118

intensity to his/her aura and it can be felt when he/she enters the room. If there is such a thing as an "average" depth to an aura, it would be in the range of a few feet. A charismatic person may have an aura which exceeds 10 or perhaps 20 feet. I have been told by some who have been in his presence, that when the Dalai Llama enters a room, his presence (aura) can be felt throughout an auditorium. The low self-esteem person may have such a low intensity aura he/she will often go totally unnoticed.

Auras and Animals

You may have known or heard about people who have an ability to attract animals. Animals are not hindered by beliefs that electro-magnetic fields do not exist. They sense these fields much more readily than humans, and the input of energy plays a significant role in the interaction between the animal and the other being.

If you approach an animal with a feeling of fear, your frequency of fear vibration is transmitted in your energy field and sensed by the animal possibly agitating the animal, or otherwise causing the animal to attack. Although there may also be aromas associated with fear, the frequency of vibration of the energy of fear is sensed by the animal.

Animals have been known to sense the change in the earth's magnetic field when an earthquake is imminent, so it only seems logical they can sense the human eloctro-magnetic field.

Awareness is the key to better living. The more one is aware of all aspects of one's own being, the better one is able to sense what is beneficial and what is harmful and make appropriate choices.

Epilogue

Ignorance is not bliss; it is simply ignorance. When considering your health, research all aspects of health. Realize standard medical practices are based on the belief that if you can convince the body into thinking something is going on, when it is not going on; or, conversely something is not going on, when it is going on, then the symptoms may be altered. It is not a guarantee the problem is corrected.

Treating symptoms will usually not get to the cause of the symptoms. Cutting out a tumor will most often not address the reason for the tumor to be growing in the first place. That does not mean the tumor should not be removed. It means that if someone is thinking for himself/herself, then he/she might want to determine if his/her working environment, living environment, eating, drinking, non-exercising, and/or smoking habits play a role in causing or triggering the expression of a genetic defect, which results in a tumor.

Remember, the body is designed to take care of itself. If symptoms are occurring, something is out of balance in the structure and/or energy systems of the body. So many of today's medications are in use because our society is accustomed to taking pills to make symptoms seem to disappear.

People want to continue to do the unhealthy things they do to their bodies and not have to pay the consequences. They do not want to change their eating habits, or smoking habits, or non-exercising habits. It is analogous to hearing some terrible sounding noise in your car engine and deciding to take care of it by turning up the stereo so you do not hear the noise any more, because the "symptom" is the noise.

My father once told me everyone dies from suicide, it is just that some forms take longer than others. How are you poisoning yourself or otherwise abusing your body?

Your health care is your choice. You can give away your power of choice or you can retain it for your own benefit.

Think about your personal goals in the area of health. Be honest in looking at what it is you have been afraid to face. In what areas have you chosen to "turn up the volume" on the stereo so you no longer "hear the noise?" What do you know now that you can choose to add or change in your life?

(One system we have not talked about, is our "belief system." Choices are made based on our beliefs. My next book will address the beliefs people have which tend to keep them from what it is they really want. My seminar, "Turn Your Dreams Into Reality" empowers people to find out what the beliefs are, discover where they were instilled and how to heal them. Contact me if you are interested in hosting a seminar in your area.)

God bless you in your search for health, and I hope you will now better understand how the body was designed and how best to support it. If you wish to contact me, you may do so at my website www.drjimw.com.

About the Author

For those of you who do not know me, a brief biography may be in order. From an educational standpoint, I attended St. Louis University for two and one-half years, majoring in math and minoring in psychology. Due to a tragic occurrence, I dropped out of school, enlisted in the Air Force, and became a weather observer. Within a year after I joined the Air Force, I received an appointment to the United States Military Academy at West Point, NY. I graduated in 1969 with a bachelor's degree in engineering. I chose to go into the Medical Service Corps of the Army as a result of three knee operations during my stay at West Point. I attended the Medical College of VA in Richmond, VA, graduating in 1972 with a master's degree in biophysics. Two years later, I suffered a heart attack while in the peak of physical condition and was medically retired from the Army. I chose to follow in my father's footsteps and become a chiropractor. I attended Logan College of Chiropractic, in the suburbs of my hometown of St. Louis, MO, and graduated with my doctor of chiropractic degree in 1979. During my chiropractic training and after graduation, I attended hundreds of hours of seminars focusing on nutrition and wellness. I studied with Dr. M. Ted Morter, Jr., D.C. to learn his "BEST" technique. I studied and trained with Mr. Ed Douglas at the "American Living Foods Institute" to learn more about "living" foods and their use in health.

I am pleased to share my knowledge with you and invite your questions. You can contact me at drjimw@drjimw.com.

An Owner's Guide

Index

Pi-Mag Water Treatment 87, 88
Prof. Irwin Korr 17-18
prosthetic devices 9
Protein Shakes 59
proteins 3, 12, 21, 24, 26, 45, 49, 50-51, 52
putrefy 2-3, 26
rancid 2-3, 13, 26, 74
Raw adrenal gland 19
recurrent meningeal nerve 100-101
Refined carbohydrates 22
Retracing 96
Running 62
Satisfaction 33
Saturated Fats 73
Skin 97
Sleep 88
small intestine 12-13
sodium 11, 54
sodium bicarbonate 11, 53
spine 7-8, 13, 18, 100, 102, 104
spleen 10, 11, 15
Sputum Test 29
stomach 12, 18, 25, 26, 40, 52, 88
Stress 'B' complex 19
subconscious belief 34-35
subluxations 100
Sucrose 21-22, 23
Swiss Soflower 97
ThalassoKea 97
Therma-Flax 115
Vitamin "A" 3

vitamin "E" 5
Walking 64
Water 13, 30, 51, 55-56, 66, 86-87, 90, 92, 106, 113-114
Yo-Yoing 59

An Owner's Guide